Dr Tran Tuan Anh

PATH TO AWAKENING
A short guide to navigate
in the meanders of the human mind

ILLUSTRATIO

Copyright © 2022 Dr TRAN Tuan Anh
All rights reserved.
ISBN : 978-2-9583609-0-0
ISBN-13 : 9782958360900

To my Masters
who showed me the way to deliverance
from the spirit

To Hiền-Mai, Huy and Hoàng
with my love and affection

To my all family
for their support and kindness

To my childhood friends from Vietnam
for their friendship that spans the years

To my friends of every moment of life
for their intellectual and spiritual sharing

To my wife Hiền-Anh
the Little Prince's Rose

To Thien-Anh Florine
who is not yet three years old
when this book came out

TABLE OF CONTENTS

Preface 11
1. Old house to be restored 13
2. Suffering is inherent
   in the human condition 16
3. Household break 20
4. The labyrinth.. 22
5. «The little prince» of St Exupery 24
6. The power of innocence................................ 27
7. We are the creators of our world 30
8. Our true masters 32
9. To each his attachment 34
10. "The lamplighter",
    the yang wood archetype 38
11. Emotional hypersensitivity: understanding
    the underlying energy mechanisms 40
12. Sufficient on yourself 43
13. The hedgehog dilemma 46
14. Let's turn our bin into a composter............. 48
15. The incredible hulk 52
16. Nothing and nobody
    will be able make us happy.......................... 54
17. When all conditions are united 56
18. Deconditioning 58
19. Reversibility 61
20. 4-wheel bike 62
21. Dr jekyll & Mr Hyde 64
22. Kill: absolute evil? 66
23. Neither good nor bad 68

24.	The usurper of love	71
25	«Detachment» is not the cure for «attachment»	73
26.	The fake-real and the real-fake Santa Claus	75
27.	Good alternative medicine	77
28.	Smile at least once an hour!	83
29.	Meditation: do not look for well-being at all costs!	85
30.	The infinite complexity of the causality	88
31.	All in one	91
32.	The importance of «zero point»	94
33.	Around the leaves corn	97
34.	A friendly world	99
35.	What are we looking for?	104
36.	A time for every step	107
37.	The gateless barrier	109
38.	The empty and the full, the visible and the invisible (1)	111
39.	The empty and the full, the visible and the invisible (2)	114
40.	The empty and the full, the visible and the invisible (3)	117
41.	Thought guides energy	120
42.	Inner harmony	123
43.	In summary, what is our life?	126
44.	Like a flower on water	127
45.	Start away from everything	130
46.	Plan everything	133
47.	Duration and flight plan	135
48.	Do not sow fear	137
49.	Revealing virus	139

50.	Back to inner source	142
51.	The plum tree in bloom	144
52.	He is free, max	146
53.	Tame life	148
54.	Awakening of consciousness	152
55.	There is only the best	153
56.	The world takes the color of your emotions	157
57.	Autumn energy	159
58.	Two simple clues	162
59.	The zen spirit is not complicated	164
60.	A wonderful illusion	166
61.	Salt statue	168
62.	The look of the others	170
63.	The «tching tchong» salad	172
64.	We are the wicked	175
65.	Little loving attitudes	177
66.	Tonglen	179
67.	The song of the rooster	182
68.	Please call me by my true names	184
69.	See the invisible	187
70.	The empty mind (heart)	189
71.	The black nose buddha	191
72.	A true donation, a true help	193
73.	The fifth dimension	195
74.	Breathe and come back at home	197
75.	Really?	199
76.	Go up	202
77.	Les vents de la vie	204
78.	Alimentary, my dear watson !	206
79.	Two special days	208
80.	A handful of salt	210

81.	Evening meditation	213
82.	Hostility	215
83.	Soul windows	217
84.	Let go	220
85.	The ordinary spirit	222
86.	Jealousy	224
87.	Primum non nocere	227
88.	The sacred dimension of our words	230
89.	Pick up the present moment	233
90.	Laugh, smile and lot of laugh	235
91.	Die is just return at home	237
92.	One of the worst experiences	240
93.	From causes to effects	243
94.	Why so much hates?	245
95.	Résolutions	248
96.	What is a chilli?	250
97.	Illumination	252
98.	The god of spinoza	255
99.	Complicated but simple and vice versa	259
100.	The ultimate truth	262
101.	Descent into hell	264
102.	It was better before!	266
103.	The right question to ask	269
104.	Balanced	272
105.	Infinite patience	275
106.	Letter to my daughter	277
Before leaving		280

PREFACE

On an ordinary day, your significant other gives you a surprise gift! Immediately, you feel surprised, happy, and satisfied: "They've been thinking of me. How touching! How thoughtful!" When you open it, however, the present isn't what you expected at all, and a wave of disappointment washes over you: "We've been together for so long... yet, they still can't remember the things that I like?" The incipient anger takes your thoughts even further: "why don't they ever listen to me; there is clearly a lack of communication." The storm of emotions can turn a seemingly positive event into negativity within seconds.

Our mind is constantly in agitation, a puppet undergoing the will of the puppet master: our ego. The ego puts the mind in all different types of situations to excite it: danger, conspiracy, manipulation, suspicion, betrayal, lack of respect, discrimination, jealousy, injustice, regret for the past, anxiety for the future ... These recurring thoughts cause significant injuries to our sense of self and act as a poison, distilled in our mind. Over time, sympathy, kindness, altruism, trust and optimism are replaced with mistrust, pessimism, and even hatred. All this leads us directly to mental and psychosomatic suffering.

Try this little exercise:

Take a deep breath. Count your breaths from 1 to 10, thinking of nothing else. Focus on the movements of your abdomen, inflating on the inhale and then deflating on the exhale.

I am willing to bet that before you get to 10, your mind is already somewhere else, lost in its erratic thoughts.

An uncontrolled mind leads directly to restlessness and then eventually to suffering. The first signs that things are about to take a turn for the worst are anxiety, rumination, fears for no valid reason, trouble sleeping, diffuse muscle and joint pain.

Regaining control of our thoughts is not an easy task. It requires years of training (possibly decades), to dissolve the ego over time so that the mind can regain true serenity and equanimity. A good direction from the start leads the practitioner to true deliverance, not to states of temporary calm with an inevitable return to restlessness. Without a clear vision of transcendent spirituality, the mind will continue to identify with its ego and return to its old destructive patterns.

In absolute terms, total liberation of the spirit can only be achieved when we have all our existential questions answered:

Who am I?
Where am I from?
What is the meaning of my life?
What will happen to me after death?

The question "Who am I?" seems nonsensical. If my ego, the "me" in myself, is taken away, what will I have left? Who would I really be?

Don't search for an answer now as you have just

begun your enlightenment journey. Take it step-by-step, day-by-day, month-by-month, year-by-year...

When spring comes the grass will sprout on its own. The truth is just like this.

Winter 2020

1
OLD HOUSE TO BE RESTORED

Our mind is like our home. Over time, it becomes the keeper of our memories, both good and bad.

At the age of twenty, although we are at the peak of our youth, our "spirit house" is not so new. During all these years, it has suffered a lot of damage from the outside, such as storms, hailstones that damage its tiles, snow that weighs on its roof, drought that cracks its walls, and even earthquakes that destroy its foundations. It could also be attacked from within, such as termites that eat its frame or weeping rot, a fungus that destroys all its woodwork. Some houses are already threatening to collapse.

I often see patients in consultation who have been suffering for forty, fifty years or more. Their house has never been maintained. They were content to hide its vices with false ceilings, to put new wallpapers or to make a facelift from time to time, to deceive themselves or to try to survive in this detestable ruin.

Let us put ourselves in the situation of a person who has just bought a (very?) old house to live in.

What would we do first? We would start by clearing the house of all its bulky items, which have been covered in dust for years.

Then, we would make it safe and livable: repair the roof by replacing the broken tiles, change the damaged frame, and consolidate the fragile places... All this work will cost us dearly, in time and energy. They are, however, necessary if we want to live happily for the rest of our lives.

I am sure we will do this for our home, but what about our minds?

When will we decide to begin restoration work, knowing that it takes years of effort and even decades to get there?

Our mind is not just a house. It is for each of us a historical monument, to be restored urgently.

Sometimes there is so much damage that it is difficult to know which end to start the work from.

The priority is already to be well in the present moment, here and now, by bringing the mind back to the essential activity of life: breathing.

As a result, the body will also be relaxed after a while.

Then, we must prepare the mind to return to our "inner child" to cherish and heal him, leaving "the battles, the conflicts... with the others" out of his thoughts.

Understanding our own needs and recognizing

our responsibility for our own suffering are the beginnings of the process of self-healing.

The latter has two phases: a correct diagnosis and then daily treatment.

The diagnosis consists in identifying the dominant emotion which remains in us since childhood (anger, attachment to pleasures, anxiety, sadness, fear), its defensive mask (the "false ceiling" that hides our sufferings), and the type of attachment of our mind (attachment to its planning, its pleasures, the needs of others, its tranquillity, or its ego).

The treatment has two phases:

- The superficial phase aims to calm the mind: relaxation, sophrology, hypnosis, meditation...

- The deep phase aims to repair the mind: awakening to spirituality, "emptying the mental trash" = training in letting go and in accepting our condition, practising compassion in thoughts, words, actions and living in full consciousness: recognizing the moment when the emotion begins to emerge to let go immediately, recognize the part of the ego in each conflict that involves us and dissolve it.

We will review these points in this book, through various reflections that will shed light on the subject from several angles.

2
SUFFERING IS INHERENT IN THE HUMAN CONDITION

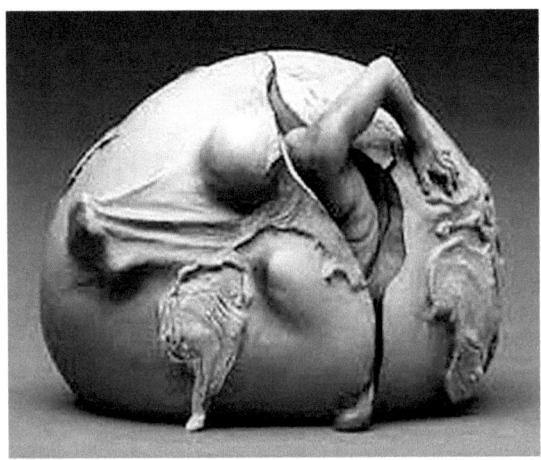

Once upon a time, there was a king who, feeling old and tired, asked his savant prime minister to send scholars to the four corners of the world to record all their observations in an encyclopaedia so that he could know the stories of humanity without leaving the palace.

Months passed, and the encyclopaedia was still not ready, but the king was getting older every day.

On his deathbed, he asked his prime minister to summarise all the tomes for him in one sentence. Then the latter approached his ear and whispered: "Humanity is suffering, your majesty!"

In my childhood, I received a Christian education

which painted a much brighter and happier picture of the world. Indeed, in the creation of the world described in the book of Genesis, the first book of the Bible, man only arrives on the sixth day, after all, that is necessary for his happiness has been created beforehand: the day and the night (light and darkness) on the first day; the sky and the waters on the second day; greenery and fruit trees on the third day; the sun, moon, and stars on the fourth day; animals, birds and fish on the fifth day; and finally the man on the sixth day to enjoy all his creations.

Genesis 1.27: "*So God created mankind in his own image, in the image of God he created them; male and female he created them.*

God blessed them and said to them, "Be fruitful and increase in number; fill the earth and subdue it. Rule over the fish in the sea and the birds in the sky and over every living creature that moves on the ground"...

Then God said, "I give you every seed-bearing plant on the face of the whole earth and every tree that has fruit with seed in it. They will be yours for food. 30 And to all the beasts of the earth and all the birds in the sky and all the creatures that move along the ground -everything that has the breath of life in it - I give every green plant for food." And it was so. God saw all that he had made, and it was very good".

Thus, man is created to be happy, because he is protected and pampered by divine power: "*The Lord is my shepherd, I lack nothing*" (Psalm 22).

Based on this principle, suffering seems to be an "anomaly" of human life. Long regarded as a consequence of sins, it has become, since the redemptive death of Christ, a test to test the solidity of faith in divine love.

In the article *"Does Suffering Make Sense?"* published in the newspaper La Croix on 06/11/2014, Father Maurice Bellet, Jesuit, wrote: *"among Christians, we find the theme of redemptive suffering, identification with the sufferings of the Savior, carrying his cross, etc...This language can go so far as to rejoice in suffering, to see in it the sign of a divine predilection - since God led his Son to the cross. "It is necessary that God loves you very much so that he tests you so much". We will say that this is to open a rather harsh perspective, since faith, instead of being immediately consolation, can become a place of trial.*

But who said faith was painless? "

In Eastern spirituality, everything seems much more pessimistic from the start.

Indeed, the Buddha's first lesson to his first five disciples after his awakening concerns suffering[1]:

"Our conditioned existence is imbued with suffering: birth is suffering, old age is suffering, illness is suffering, death is suffering, being united with what we do not love is suffering, to be separated from what one loves is suffering - and, finally, the five aggregates of attachment (matter, sensation, perception, mental formations and consciousness) *are also sufferings"*.

Thus, suffering is inherent in the human condition. We all suffer all the time, to varying degrees. This is not an "anomaly" of life but its reality!

Seen from this angle, each moment of well-being is a time of respite that we must appreciate to the maximum.

---

[1] The Four Noble Truths taught by the Buddha during his first sermon, called "Benares Sermon" or "The Setting in Motion of the Wheel of the Dharma Sutta (Buddhist teaching)"

We can illustrate the difference between these two thoughts by the meteorological metaphor.

With Western thought, we believe that we live in a southern climate where the weather is always good. However, it rains so often that we think we are unlucky and spend our time hoping that "after rain, comes fair weather ". By seeing so few sunny days, sadness and depression will set in.

With Eastern thought, we know that we live in a northern climate where it rains very often.

Therefore, whenever the weather is good, we make the most of the sun by accepting that "after fair weather, comes rain". It is a realistic view that seems pessimistic at first but helps a lot to relativize suffering in the future.

Apart from physical pain, suffering is the crystallisation of emotions that have been repressed and reserved for an exceedingly long time. Therefore, it cannot be easily disappeared by temporary relaxation, or by an escape to material pleasures or hard work...

Its nature needs to be, as much as the recipe for transformation. Indeed, suffering is not totally negative, on the contrary.

It is the breeding ground for awakening. Without it, we do not seek to free ourselves from it by tending towards a transcendent spirituality.

Joys and sorrows are two sides of the same coin. A good gardener sees beautiful flowers in the compost of his garden. Let us know how to transform the sufferings of our past into a life awakened to those of others.

3
HOUSEHOLD BREAK

Close your eyes for a moment.

No longer look at the societies that make you bristle, the people who dislike you, the injustices that revolt you, the events that worry you, your past that saddens you... You have already spent a lot, even too much time contemplating them.

Just take a little moment for yourself. Close your eyes and turn your gaze inward. Turn on the light there and inspect.

You might see a little kid there who is angry, who breaks his friends' toys because they are more beautiful than his, or who cries because he feels so lonely when he is still unable to suffice for himself, or that he is simply afraid because others seem so threatening to him...

Her room is cluttered with garbage cans that have not been emptied for a long time, filled with resentments, disappointments, frustrations...

How long has it been since you let him fend for himself, without care, without affection... just watching and judging the behaviour of others?

So close your eyes just a moment and breathe, come back to yourself. Your inner child is in dire need of you.

Take him in your arms.

Help him tidy up his room.

Empty her emotional garbage cans.

4
THE LABYRINTH

Our life sometimes feels like a labyrinth. We go around in circles without precise direction and we often find ourselves facing dead ends.

When my patients compare their lives to this picture, I always ask them: "Do you know how we get out of the maze of our lives in the safest and fastest way?"

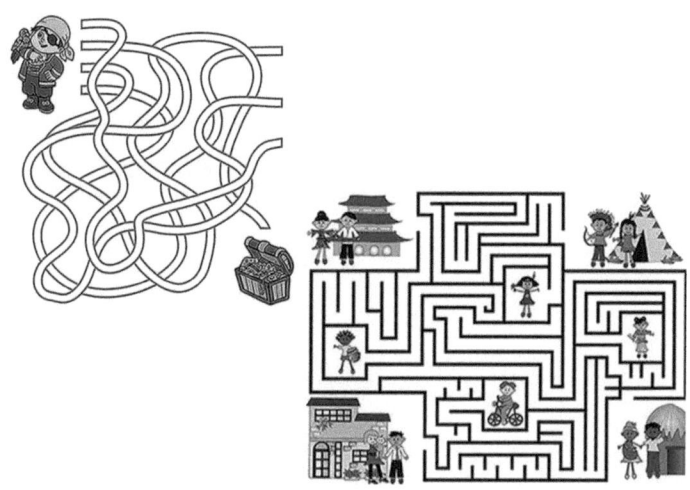

When we were kids, we all played these maze games where you have to help Jack the pirate find his treasure or little Peter return home. Even a 5-year-old can find the right path! Why? Because he is above the labyrinth and thus sees the points of departure and arrival.

A labyrinth is only a problem when we are in it, not above it. Therefore, the safest and fastest way to get out of the maze is to elevate ourselves to a spirituality that gives meaning to our life.

Jack the pirate or the little Peter, it is our ego which constantly demands respect, affection, love, loyalty, wealth, social position... all these needs which depend on the goodwill of others . It is the source of our disappointments and dead ends.

We are not our ego.

It is just our avatar, mask, and illusion.

Let us leave it in its maze and rise!

5
"THE LITTLE PRINCE" OF ST EXUPERY

When tidying up my bookcase, I took a photo of my book collection "Le petit prince" by St Exupéry in different languages and editions.

My mother gave me the French version of this book when I was 10 years old. I still remember my first impression after reading it. I found the story very weird and uninteresting.

And then, with every re-read at the age of 12, 14, 17... and then again and again in adulthood, I discovered new life lessons, and it became my first book of Western wisdom.

This is the second book translated into the world after the Bible. So, on each trip, I looked for the version (s) published in the country visited.

Those who know me give me the edition of their country, making me travel like a little prince around the world. Today I was able to assemble a small collection of around 70 copies of my favourite book.

When we mention it, I have the impression that only a few passages have aroused the reader's interest, such as those of the meeting with the fox or with the rose. In fact, this book is an awakening treasure for the mind.

The little prince is our child's soul, who sets out to discover the world of "grown-ups" whose life has caused the loss of primordial innocence. They are represented by characters on their planet:

. "The King", thirsty for power

. "The Vanity", swollen with vainness

. "The Drinker", who loses all sense of life

. "The Businessman", feverish with possessions

. "The lamplighter", prisoner of duty and instructions

. "The Geographer", locked in the beliefs of knowledge without ever experiencing one himself.

He teaches us to maintain our planet (= spirit) so as not to let strong emotions overwhelm it. He regularly sweeps his volcanoes, even the one that is extinct: *"If they are well swept, the volcanoes burn slowly and regularly, without eruptions"*.

He remains vigilant to the emergence of bad thoughts, symbolised by baobabs, which initially appear as lovely twigs among the good grasses. They can even be confused with roses! However, if allowed to grow, these thoughts will turn into inappropriate words and attitudes that can harm. The roots of the baobab then puncture the planet and cause it to burst.

He also experiences the first feelings with a rose that has accidentally arrived on his planet, which, after being tamed by his heart will become his only rose among thousands of others.

On his journey to earth, he meets the author, stranded in the desert, and reminds him of the importance of this lost childhood innocence, as well as the value of love that can light up all the stars in the sky.

He learns the true values of everything from his master, a sharp-eyed fox who can see the invisible.

He finally experiences death, which is not an end, but a simple return to where he came from, immortal.

In the next chapters, I will approach some passages of the book with an oriental vision to help you discover the great wisdom of St Exupéry, an author dear to my heart.

6
THE POWER OF INNOCENCE

St Exupéry's *"The Little Prince"* begins with a story from his childhood, in which the author showed "grown-ups" the image of the "closed" boa swallowing an elephant.

Since the latter only saw a hat, he was forced to redo another drawing with an "open" boa showing the elephant inside.

As an adult, he used this image as a test:

"Whenever I met [a grown-up] who seemed to me at all clear-sighted, I tried the experiment of showing him my Drawing Number One, which I have always kept. I would try to find out if this was a person with a true understanding. But whoever it was, he, or

she would always say: "That is a hat" then I would never talk to that person about boa constrictors, or primaeval forests, or stars. I would bring myself down to his level. I would talk to him about the bridge, golf, politics, and neckties. And the grown-up would be greatly pleased to have met such a sensible man."

It is the phrase "*I would bring myself down to his level*" that makes this passage extraordinary. Here are "grown-ups" treated like children who do not understand much!

Yes, we think that as grown-ups, far smarter than children, we know how to distinguish right from wrong and we take care of serious and concrete things, such as our fortune and our career, by putting them in front of the rest.

In reality, we are regressing! We lose a great power, that of innocence, which provides a subtle vision to see the essential value of everything.

We doubt everything, condemn everyone, and make our world so grey that even rainbows are no longer coloured. Kindness has become stupidity ("too good, too dumb") and cunning has become intelligence. Our gaze has lost all subtlety. We see enemies, bad people, but are unable to see their suffering behind their behaviour, as well as our own suffering through our skin reactions. We see the benefits for ourselves in an operation, but we are blind to the losses suffered by others.

However, becoming an adult does not mean turning into "a grown-up".

The proof: the author, as an adult, will tell you about serious things, such as "*boa constrictors, primaeval forests, or stars*", if he recognizes the lucid child who remains in you.

So now and then, come back to the "closed boa" image and look at it closely. If you see an elephant there, all is not lost. Then you will be ready for the big trip, at the next wild bird migration.

And do not forget to carefully keep the secret revealed by St Exupéry at the end of his book: *"It is only with the heart that one can see rightly; what is essential is invisible to the eye"*.

7
WE ARE THE CREATORS OF OUR WORLD

Thirty people spent two days of seminars together in a hotel conference room. Apart from the time for the presentations, they had meals together, took breaks together, and talked a lot together. After the seminar, each participant is asked to describe everything they have experienced during these two days, their perception of the atmosphere, the people they have met, the experiences they have accumulated...

No one describes the same thing. For Mr N., Mr P. did not even exist, although he was sitting only a few feet away from him. Although Mrs B. found the seminar extraordinary with nice people, Mrs M. had not liked it at all, only meeting petty and obtuse people. Strangely, it was like they did not live in the same world during these two days.

If we extrapolate this little experience to all of humanity, we realise that there are as many different worlds as there are people. Indeed, each of us creates his[2] own universe, like a director who makes his film: we choose the characters who appear there, the atmosphere that reigns there (comedy or tragedy, love or hate, serenity or fear, happy end or tragic end...), the rules and paths that all these actors must follow, including ourselves. No matter how much we say we are following divine or human law, we willfully change it to serve our interests when the opportunity arises, sometimes blaming the tempting devil, alcohol, or drugs to justify.

Our illusion is to believe that the other worlds should take a model from ours which serves as a reference. We also forget that each of us is the sole creator of the Universe in which he lives and is therefore solely responsible for everything that is there, the atmosphere that reigns there.

We all dream of a cleaner, better, more equal, more equitable and more united world. Let us start by changing our own, reducing our mental waste, slowing down our pace of life so as not to forget the essentials, basing our thoughts, words and actions on compassion to flower our hearts and those of others. This is the starting point of a new world.

---

[2] His / her

8
OUR TRUE MASTERS

Usually, when we are asked who our guide is, our reference teacher in life, the answer is often "God", "Jesus", "Buddha" or "my conscience of good and evil" and "love for the next one "...

If this was true, our world would be at peace, there would be no more wars, conflicts of interest, various struggles, disputes, discrimination, or aggression.

Let us be honest with ourselves: our real masters, those who can submit to us, are our own emotions.

When we are angry, all our references disappear and we blindly follow what our master "anger" tells us to do: hurtful or even insulting words, regrettable actions for the future, self-destruction...

When we desperately seek pleasure, this ephemeral "joy", our master pushes us to greed:

addiction, cheating, deception, lies, even aggression, theft... to have more money, more power, more satisfaction in life, even to the detriment of others.

When we are anxious, our teacher guides us to demand and put pressure on those around us to compensate for our inability to be sufficient in ourselves.

When we are sad, our master isolates us in our misfortunes, and our sufferings and cuts us off from others so that we cannot get by with their helpers.

When we are afraid, our teacher leads us in the perpetual flight of the world perceived as threatening or transforms us into "skinned alive" who suffer endless victimisation, feeling obligated to constantly fight to be well regarded.

Every day, I witness unnecessary suffering resulting from the disaster of badly tamed emotions: family conflicts, professional conflicts, deep discomfort that nothing seems to be saving... not to mention their repercussions on the body: insomnia, anxiety-depressive syndrome, addiction, tendino-muscular and joint pains, self-destructive diseases...

If there is one struggle that is utterly worth it, it is the one that frees us from the grip of our emotions on our lives.

It is difficult because the sufferings of our past, our bad experiences and our memories tend to add fuel to the fire to nourish them, to continue to exert their hold on us through our ego.

It is difficult because bad habits in our behaviour have become our survival reflexes, even if their nature is perverse and harmful.

Recognizing our true masters and our condition as slaves is the first step towards delivering our deep suffering.

9
TO EACH HIS ATTACHMENT

While Eastern spirituality recognizes attachment as the factor that creates and sustains suffering, we do not all have the same attachments.

They are in fact our defensive mask to hide an underlying overflowing emotion, difficult to control for an untrained mind.

Thus, there are five main types of attachment, related to the five energetic movements of the body and their corresponding five emotions:

1. The **Wood-**type:

The emotion of the Wood-type is anger.

Its defensive mask is the dedication to planning, programming and perfection (including the little details that are very unimportant to others). They like planners, notes, labels, and pens of all colours to keep things organised. When their plans do not go as planned, their anger comes out and can be explosive. In regression, they can stress themselves to the point of "drowning in a glass of water" and go into an obsessive state.

Their main suffering is the difficulty in letting go.

2. The **Fire-**type:

The emotion of the Fire-type is joy.

Joy being fleeting, the Fire-type fears the void when it is gone. His defensive mask is a race for ephemeral pleasures that risks leading him to addiction (sex, drugs, work, games…).

He is motivated by the desire for possession and does not cope with frustration. He often runs behind "several hares" at the same time to always have a "pleasure-option" ready to be used in his pocket. In regression, he may make compulsive purchases or exhaust himself in satisfying his frustrations by the race for exciting things. Depression or addiction is not far away.

3. The **Earth-**type:

The emotion of the Earth-type is anxiety.

To justify his constant anxiety, he becomes attached to the needs of others, at the risk of neglecting his own needs. He is motivated by helping others. It makes him feel useful and selfless.

In decline, he expects a return from those he has helped and may suffer from their indifference to him. He can sink into exhaustion or even depression when dependence on others exceeds his ability to give.

4. The **Metal**-type:

The emotion of the Metal-type is sadness.

In order not to feel it constantly, the Metal-type buries it in the back of his mind and does not manifest his emotions on the outside. He is attached to the tranquillity of his inner world which he wants to preserve at all costs. Introverted and slow, he limits the approaches of others and prefers to observe the world around him to learn all the lessons. In regression, he can cut himself off from those around him to live alone, suffering from links that are impossible to establish with others because of this distance.

5. The **Water**-type:

The emotion of the Water-type is fear.

He lives in a feeling of permanent insecurity (fear of missing out, being betrayed, abandoned, and being despised...)

To hide the pervasive fear in his mind due to lack of self-confidence, the Water-type has two defence systems: fleeing from situations considered threatening or confronting immediately to nip danger in the bud.

He blows up his ego to prove to others that he fears nothing and no one. Often suspicious and behaving like a "skinned alive" with a spirit of protest, he fights against what he sees as treason, disloyalty, or injustice. In regression, he can see conspiracies against him from all sides and thus creates a climate of conflict with those around him.

Thus, we have within each of us a particular type of attachment, with the suffering associated with it.

It is by knowing ourselves and by sympathising with the emotions of others that we will be able to find the right words and actions, live in harmony with each other and bring peace to the world.

10
"THE LAMPLIGHTER", THE YANG WOOD ARCHETYPE

In the world of St Exupéry's *"The Little Prince"*, if you can see the stars twinkling at night, it is thanks to street light lighters that turn them back on each night, then turn them off when the day arrives.

"When he lights his streetlamp, it is as if he brought one more star to life or one flower. When he puts out his lamp, he sends the flower, or the star, to sleep. That is a beautiful occupation. And since it is beautiful, it is truly useful".

One day, when the little prince arrived at the

smallest planet where only one lamplighter lives, his astonishment was total. With his planet spinning faster and faster, he was forced to turn his lamppost on and off every minute. However, not being able to deviate from the instructions, he continued to carry out this work even without having time to sleep and chained a series of "good morning-good evening" to his visitor.

"*Those are the orders. There is nothing to understand, said the lamplighter. Orders are orders*".

According to traditional Chinese medicine theories, this character has the emotional profile of the Wood-Yang subtype. To fight against the anger he constantly has in him as a sleeping volcano, he will organise his defence by planning his life around a personal notion of perfection and blamelessness, based on rules and principles, even protocols. His main suffering is his difficulty in letting go. When he comes up with his plan, he sticks to the smallest detail aiming for perfection and can drown in a glass of water. He then becomes obsessive.

As he left this planet, [the little prince] "*breathed a sigh of regret, and said to himself, again: That man is the only one of them all whom I could have made my friend. But his planet is indeed too small. There is no room on it for two people. . .*".

Therefore, if you recognize yourself in the image of the "lamplighter," be mindful of others, especially those who may not understand or buy into your planning. By absolutely seeking perfection in the realisation of your projects, you privilege reason over feelings and gradually shrink your planet, until you are the only inhabitant who could find space there.

11
EMOTIONAL HYPERSENSITIVITY: UNDERSTANDING THE UNDERLYING ENERGY MECHANISMS

Psychology publications often speak of hypersensitive people, who suffer from experiencing their emotions "on edge", arousing incomprehension from those around them, as one type of character.

However, after years of observing my peers, I have identified mainly three different types of hypersensitive people. They each correspond to a separate energy weakness, with different emotional defence behaviours.

The first is the **Water**-type.

His main emotional weakness, being fear and lack of self-confidence, he has learned from a young age to be wary of others, of their fine words which might hide unpleasant intentions, of their promises and potential betrayals. For this reason, he systematically "scans" his interlocutors to detect their possible hidden intentions and estimates the degree of confidence that he can have in them. Over the years, he feels endowed with a special intuition, able to read behaviour and foresee conspiracies. However, his scanner being too sensitive, he will feel attacked, judged, or hurt in front of certain innocuous facts or words which do not target him personally and will suffer uselessly. The **Water-Yin** subtype flees from a threatening situation. Conversely, the Water-Yang subtype behaves like a "skinned alive" which reacts violently in the face of injustice and betrayal. He likes to wear the image of the vigilante fighting to restore justice to his own standards His emotional hypersensitivity stems from his fear of the world around him, in which he lives with a constant feeling of insecurity.

Another type of hypersensitive person is the **Fire-Yin** subtype. The emotion of Fire is joy, but in the Fire-Yin subtype, the energy of Fire is so weak that the joy of life finds it difficult to take hold in one's life. Inhabited by a great emptiness in its heart, the Yin Fire desires what is not available, difficult to obtain, or even beyond reach. It could be a lost, impossible, idealised and unattainable love or even a desire for a child unfulfilled by sterility. They are often artists (poets, writers, actors, dancers, singers, painters...) who have a great sense of aesthetics and who have the particularity of sublimating their suffering in their works. The more they suffer, the more their works are beautiful, even extraordinary. They see themselves as special beings who find it difficult to integrate into society with its banal codes and standards.

Their love life is often a psychodrama as they desire a love that is as flamboyant as a flash in the pan while being as enduring as a coal fire. The emotional hypersensitivity of the Yin Fire manifests itself through its yearning for the impossible. However, if he finally gets what he has tirelessly pursued, he will find it so commonplace that his pain could not be eased.

The third type of hypersensitive person is the Earth-type. To alleviate his permanent anxiety, he will turn his attention to the needs of those around him, at the risk of forgetting his own needs. Armed with his altruism, he embarks on his fight for the poor and the forgotten (homeless, migrants...) by trying to change their living conditions. Sometimes he chooses to engage in long and difficult processes of helping others without necessary resources. This can lead to exhaustion and depression with a feeling of worthlessness.

The **Earth**-type emotional hypersensitivity is because he is already naturally sensitive to the suffering of others. By adding his own, his capacities are exceeded and leave him in an insoluble paradox "I need to help others to be well, but I am incapable of it, therefore I need to be helped, but it doesn't do me any good".

Altogether, emotional hypersensitivity has many natures and each has its remedies. It is by properly understanding the underlying energetic process that each person can be offered a work of their own self-healing that will help them cope.

12
SUFFICIENT ON YOURSELF

We expect a lot from the world around us: understanding, care, help, joy, love, good appreciation, respect, loyalty, fidelity, justice ... And we are frequently disappointed, sad, or angry because his answers often do not match our expectations.

Over time, some of us become embittered, suspicious, even unfriendly, or aggressive with others. Others become dependent on the appreciation of those around them, the "likes" of virtual friends on social networks to feel less empty and have more self-confidence.

Indeed, we are not closed universes, limited by the border of the self. We constantly interact with our environment and those around us. We need the sun, rain, the earth, animals, plants, and our fellows to subsist, and this since the dawn of time. We borrow some things from them and provide them with some others. It is symbiosis: everything is One in perpetual inter-existence.

This is also true in human relationships. To be happy, we need a serene, peaceful, harmonious atmosphere with others. However, this condition is seriously threatened if we carry out a self "border closure" and a "declaration of war" with anything considered anti-self.

Let us examine our minds. This is because we are not sufficient on our own.

Being self-sufficient does not mean being arrogant and standing above others, on the contrary.

Like a beggar who has just realised that he is immensely rich, this sudden awakening will reveal to us that there is no need to fight for respect or to prove our worth. We will no longer need to put pressure on those around us to impose admiration, care, and even love on them. We will love ourselves enough that our image is never tarnished in our eyes in the face of hurtful criticism from others. Therefore, we no longer behave like perpetual victims of the "wickedness" of others.

We have enough to no longer be jealous of the happiness of those around us. We will be able to give them without expecting anything in return, not even a thank you.

And above all, when our ego is transparent, we can alone go through thunderstorms and storms, without fear and without suffering too much. We will become an inexhaustible source where everyone can find comfort, a solid rock for those around us, but without pride or feeling of being indispensable.

Before, we did not want to be trampled on. Now, becoming transparent without ego, we no longer suffer from this problem.

Thus, being self-sufficient while remaining in harmony with others is a spiritual maturity that can only be acquired with daily awakening and training of the mind.

13
THE HEDGEHOG DILEMMA

18th-century German philosopher Arthur Schopenhauer used this analogy to refer to the difficulties of the human relationship: a group of hedgehogs seeking to come together to share their warmth in cold weather. However, if they are too close to each other, they will hurt each other with their thorns. Too far away, they cannot warm up.

One day, a patient told me about the dilemma she had just experienced: divorced for several years, she was looking for a soul mate to break her loneliness. By chance, she met a man who wanted to commit to her for a life together. It was at this point that she entered such intense stress that made her recoil. She feared he would discovered her flaws and cut their relationship off, which would hurt her even more.

Fear is often the root of our contradictions. We are afraid of loneliness but also afraid to disappoint, afraid of being suffocated by the other, afraid of being wrong, of being betrayed, abandoned, afraid of showing ourselves without a mask, of being disappointed by another failure, fear of the complications created by the new situation… What thorns that would hurt each other if we got too close to each other!

This fear arises out of the self-preservation reflex of the self. It makes us wary of others and pushes us to stay away from them. As a result, relationships become cold and distant, losing all the heat necessary for their development.

Sometimes, to achieve balance, it is necessary for us to overcome the fear of renewal, to go beyond the pseudo-"comfort zone", and take the risk of trusting others and assuming the consequences of our choices.

Every birth begins with pain. All maturity goes through hardship. All freedom requires self-surrender.

Without it, the germ will never become a tree, nor the chrysalis a butterfly.

14
LET'S TURN OUR BIN INTO A COMPOSTER

A patient had made me read the story of her life through a biography written after multiple steps of spiritual research as well as a long therapy that allowed her to rebuild herself and to be happy today.

It is a blood-curdling life story, as it expresses the deep fear she had felt from childhood, where untoward events and malicious people seemed to relentlessly revolve around her.

Her life was a real pain. Insecure family history and atmosphere: raped in childhood by her mother's lover, so she couldn't reveal the affair to her parents, repeated failures in her studies and her various married lives, she wrote: "*I am going through terrible depression, constantly devaluing me, I feel empty inside a body, that no word can rehabilitate. I feel* as bad as I think I am [...] I only have one desire: to disappear... ".

From there, a process of "self-harm" is initiated: "*I realised that I have become the victim of what my defence mechanism has put in place. I have become my own tormentor when my devaluing thoughts lock me into a pattern of belief that no one can understand me and that I am not worthy of being loved [...] At any time, I know I can be the prey of such a thought and that giving it importance and identifying myself with it amounts to provoking a chain of painful events [...] In fact, I realise that I have identified with the desperation of my loneliness [...] Devaluation is pernicious. She keeps me in a vicious circle, where the patterns are repeated endlessly, without my being able to change them, even if I want to [...] It seems that I always choose my companions reinforcing the negative image I have of myself. Each of them reflects the bridles of my hidden history, through their own unresolved experience.*"

From an energetic point of view, this patient is of the **Water**-type. Her dominant emotion is fear. Since her childhood, the latter is constantly nourished by a spirit that devalues itself, losing all self-confidence and trying to defend itself by erroneous mechanisms which, instead of freeing it, make it sink further into despair.

Her inner child is lost in the middle of unemptied trash cans for a very long time: "*I begin to tell myself that I developed with all the annoyance and sadness felt as a child in my parents, through violence and grief, education , their inconsistency, ignorance, and above all by a lack of unconditional regard. Rape accentuated this feeling of loneliness and developed, to the point of identifying myself, with guilt, shame, low self-esteem, agonizing insecurity, the inability to recognize and satisfy my needs, to be listening to my emotions, my academic difficulties including memorization, my inability to receive, my romantic failures, my professional problems, my difficulties integrating into a group, my eating disorders, my insomnia, my back pain and muscular, a subtle tendency to masochism, depression, mental confusion."*

And then, one day, through a clean spiritual path and a lot of effort, she found a way to deliver herself through a rebirth: transforming her "trash" spirit into a "composter".

She writes "*I am more able to listen from the inside to what my emotions are telling me, and the needs that go with them instead of listening to the outside who feels they know better than me what I feel and think. Eventually, my references become internal, more and more alive in me than any other feelings. Thus, I slowly integrate the idea that I am a full-fledged being, who has the right to live, worthy of respect and love.*

Recognizing and finally appreciating my values, I venture to express them more freely, calmly, and with a sense that it is good. Through this freed space, I have the feeling of resuming the course of my life with the pleasure of feeling normal, the notion of free will takes on meaning, the feeling of being myself with an impression of being integrated, connected to others, to the universe, with growing respect, dignity and energy".

This testimony is so extraordinary that I asked his permission to share it with you. For once, I do not have much to add.

When the limits of our ego evaporate, allowing us to become universes open once again and connected to others, we will no longer suffer on our own in silence.

On the compost from the waste of our sufferings will finally grow the flowers of awakening to compassion, for oneself and others, from the seeds of infinite love.

15
THE INCREDIBLE HULK

A patient once confided to me: "*It's as if in me there are two people living together. One is clear and reasonable, understands everything, knows what to do and what to avoid, what is right and what is wrong. The other appears when emotions take hold of me. I do not understand what is happening to me: my head knows that it is absurd and that I am wrong, but a strong impulse pushes me to say bad things, to threaten, to insult, to choose violence, to lie... When I calmed down, I was so sorry for the damage caused to those around me that I was afraid that I would be let down*".

His testimony reminds me of the Hulk, a superhero created by Marvel in the 60s.

This is the story of Dr Bruce Banner, a shy scientist

irradiated with gamma rays, who hides within him a devastating monster with a childish mind. The latter only asks to be left in peace. During times of stress or intense anger, Doctor Banner metamorphoses into this colossal green-skinned creature, the Hulk, who possesses phenomenal strength and carries a rage he cannot control. This rage has been present in him since his youth when, as a little boy, he was beaten by his father and saw his mother die under the blows of the latter.

The Hulk is so gigantic that he overshoots Banner's petite stature, cracks all his clothes, and sweeps everything in his path, fearful of no bullets, cars, or obstacles.

In fact, we all have an incredible Hulk inside of us. The heavier our past, with traumatic after-effects and a lack of love, the bigger, stronger, and more ruthless our monster is. It is called "ego". Even oversized, he is in fact only a small child who suffers, who is afraid, often cries for help, needs to be recognized and demands justice for himself constantly, not being sufficient for himself.

He needs to be reassured and loved but scares others so much that he constantly creates a void of desolation around him.

Maybe it is time for each of us to take care of our true loving and peaceful natures like Doctor Banner and let the Hulk know that there is no need to wake up anymore.

It takes spiritual awakening, regular training of the mind and a lot of patience, but the rewards are well worth the effort.

16
NOTHING AND NOBODY WILL BE ABLE TO MAKE US HAPPY

This morning, a patient confided in me: *"I don't understand why I have everything I need to be happy: a wife and children who love me, a job I have chosen, a comfortable home, an above-average lifestyle and yet I'm not happy. I think I had never been happy since I was a child"*.

I replied: "Indeed, you can 'have' everything without 'being'. Happiness is just a state of mind".

The followers of positive psychology believe that it is enough to align a series of pleasures that will follow one another day after day to fill the void of existence and bring happiness there. Unfortunately, this feeling of happiness is very fleeting and fragile because it depends on the conditions in which we live. If we count on them, the day they change (unemployment, divorce, illness, accident...), our feeling of happiness will collapse, quickly replaced by frustrations and regrets, making the bed of suffering.

Some of us are eagerly awaiting true love. As in a fairy tale, we hope that the dreamed person, with his[3] passionate love for us will manage to fill all our voids, our gaps and make us happy.

The reality is often quite different. We will put so much hope (and therefore pressure) on the loved one that he will eventually run away to regain his freedom.

If we are not sufficient on our own, nothing and no one can make us happy.

Happiness is nothing out of the ordinary. It is just a vision of life, a creation of the mind.

If we create paradise, it will be present everywhere, in each blade of grass, each stone, each animal, each gesture, each smile... It could even be present in trials, hard moments of life, like a little sugar sweetening up a cup of bitter coffee.

If we create hell, it will also be omnipresent, even in the most wonderful landscapes, the most magnificent palaces, on the most beautiful beaches in the world, in the most benevolent hearts and the most passionate loves.

Nothing and no one can make us happy if we do not take the trouble to create a little paradise there.

---

[3] his / her

17
WHEN ALL CONDITIONS ARE UNITED

Every connoisseur knows it. It takes a lot of favourable conditions for wine to be good: the type of grape variety that corresponds to the geographical area in question, the optimal climatic conditions: neither too much water nor too little, no hail, enough light and the exact right amount of heat, a lot of work in the vineyard by the winegrower, winemaking know-how, ideal wine storage conditions...

When all these conditions are met, we can obtain a grand cru, a vintage that will last for years while gradually increasing in value, a sure value.

Our relationships with others are like fine wine. They require a lot of care, attention, and favourable situations to grow, become strong and fulfilled.

However, we often forget that we have the power

to create these good conditions, but also the power to destroy them by our words, our actions, often guided by our uncontrollable emotions.

Today I would like to focus on the fear, the emotion that takes us away from healthy and constructive relationships. Lack of self-confidence makes us overly suspicious of others, their looks, and their judgments. We want to show them that we are not afraid of them. We then act like the Donkey in La Fontaine's fable who dresses in lion skin to scare away other animals. The worst part is that we are unable to then recognize our responsibility for the desertion of our loved ones and accept the consequences. We continue to think that life is unfair to us and always puts us in front of mean and ungrateful people.

Personal development specialist Dale Carnegie once wrote: *"If you want honey, don't kick the beehive!"*.

A nail stuck in a post always leaves a mark, even when removed. Hurtful words, even frank and fair ones, can create irreparable damage.

This is the law of cause and effect. Every effect has a cause, to be considered carefully with a calm and clear mind, unaffected by emotions or the demand to satisfy the ego.

If love and compassion become the basis of all words, all actions, then the conditions will always be optimal for obtaining "vintage" relationships that will stand the test of time without deteriorating.

18
DECONDITIONING

Do you know the monkey theorem?

It is a fable describing an imaginary experiment carried out on a group of monkeys. Five chimpanzees are isolated in a room where there is a banana at the top of a ladder. As soon as one monkey begins to climb the ladder, the others automatically receive a cold shower.

Quickly, chimpanzees learn that they must not climb the ladder if they are to avoid being watered. The shower is then deactivated, but the chimpanzees retain the experience gained and do not attempt to approach the ladder.

One of the monkeys is replaced by a new one. When the latter approaches the ladder, the other monkeys attack him violently and push him away. When a second chimpanzee is replaced, he too is attacked while trying to climb the ladder, including by the first replacement monkey.

The experiment is continued until all the first chimpanzees that had undergone the cold showers are all replaced. Yet the monkeys still do not attempt to climb the ladder to reach the banana. And if one of them tries it nevertheless, he is punished by the others, without anyone knowing why it is forbidden even though none of them has ever had a cold shower.

This phenomenon is called "conditioning". Since our childhood, we are conditioned by our parents, by the society in which we live (with its culture, its mentalities, and its rules), by religion, by different ideologies and currents of thought... The methods of conditioning are often based on fear (fear of sins, fear of not pleasing God, fear of such regimes or such ideas, fear of failure which leads to poverty, fear of the gaze of others, fear of disappointing...) and on the feelings of shame and guilt.

Like everything, this conditioning has two effects. Its positive effect can shape us into successful, independent, and responsible adults who are useful to society and to others. On the other hand, its negative effect can lead us towards a single thought without discernment, towards erroneous certainties which guide our life towards suffering, towards feelings of shame of not being able to reach our ideal, even of guilt of not being "in standards".

Buzz Aldrin, the American cosmonaut, has suffered all his life from being "only" the second man to set foot on the moon. His father had always told him: "Only the first counts!".

Therefore, one of the key stages in the deliverance of our spirit is its deconditioning.

This is a difficult and painful step for many people,

but the results are greatly beneficial in the long run.

Deconditioning begins with a change in thinking, from duality to unity: everything, every event always has two sides, light and dark, intimately linked. An equanimous mind accepts whatever comes its way, whatever its aspect, positive or negative.

So, if we get to "see the lotus in the mud and the mud in the lotus," our minds will become equanimous.

We will free ourselves from our torments when we stop "loving these because they meet our standards" and "hating these because they are different from our norms".

An equanimous mind can weather all storms and face all kinds of situations because it is free from any prior conditioning.

Better, it will free us from our own demons: our fears and our guilt that have always chained us.

19
REVERSIBILITY

The leather jacket of my mind lacked skin,
Flayed alive.
Smile in front but suffer in it; A boat
Adrift.
Through thick and thin; A mask
So perfect
My spirit, alone, weary of war
Was crying.
And then time passing,
Joys and sorrows washed away.
Everything passes.
The end will come one day,
Without preface.
Return your jacket, it is time!
Interior side.
Suffer in front, inevitable,
But smile inside,
Happiness.

20
4-WHEEL BIKE

Spiritual life is like a child. It must grow up and become mature, otherwise, it will remain infantile.

When we were kids learning to ride a bike, the extra two wheels were so invaluable. They made it easier for us to sit up and ride without losing our balance.

However, in adulthood, they become obstacles. If we do not remove them, we cannot move forward smoothly and quickly.

During my childhood, I had received a Christian education in the rigorous rules: the good deeds to be performed, the sins to be avoided. It allowed me to build a solid foundation at the beginning of my spiritual journey. Prayer has supported me in difficult times of doubt and fear. The catechism gave a good direction to my life and endowed me with an altruistic vision filled with love for others. Everything seemed solid and perfect.

I remember when I questioned the concepts of my religious education. It was seen by those around me as if I were removing those extra wheels to ride only with two main wheels. How many spiritual guides from my childhood advised me to drop this crazy idea: with such speed and without security, I risk ending up in a ravine and losing (eternal) life there! And that is what happened.

Strangely enough, like a seed that had died in good soil, my spiritual life was reborn as a small plant, which grew with the sun and closed its leaves at night to drink the dew. Slowly it took root and grew.

I finally understood that belief is based solely on trusting the words, the teachings we had received from the elders.

To grow, spirituality needs our own awakening, our own experiences from our practices, our mistakes, our falls, our pains, and our perseverance. It will become ours and nothing can take it away from us.

However, we will have to accept this crossing of doubt, this work without a safety net, sometimes with the fear in our stomachs of going into the unknown.

If you are worried about falling into the ravine, do not remove those two extra wheels.

21
DR JEKYLL & MR HYDE

London 1886. Dr Jekyll is a philanthropist, full of kindness towards others.

However, he hides a terrible secret: he is inhabited by an evil and vicious character, Mr. Hyde, who grows inside him and over the years transforms him into a ruthless murderer.

Dr Jekyll, therefore, spends his life developing an elixir that allows him to separate definitively from Mr Hyde to find the good that is in him. Unfortunately, Hyde is growing and taking up more and more space.

To neutralize him once and for all, Jekyll commits suicide. Good died with evil.

I have always enjoyed using Western literature to illustrate notions of Eastern spirituality.

Since our childhood, the influence of religion is such that we struggle with all our might to reverse evil and improve good.

It is an excellent choice for the moral education of our children, where the good-bad distinction will allow them to start well in life and to grow into loving and responsible people.

However, in adulthood, the complexity of human-to-human relationships and their inexorable evolution blur the line between good and evil.

The worst consequence of our childhood "formatting" is that we often side with the "good" and see those who do not think like us to be on the other side.

It is a dual, discriminating thought, a source of divisions and wars. Thus, by wanting to annihilate the night, we have annihilated the day at the same time.

Man is not mean to man. He simply suffers and often chooses the worst possible solution: fighting his neighbour. He forgets that the latter is not the source of his suffering, unlike the real culprit, his mistaken vision, which obscures his benevolence.

Non-discriminating thinking is based on another non-Manichean duality, the Yin-Yang duality. Thus, darkness (Yin) and light (Yang) are inseparable.

The existence of one conditions the existence of the other. This is the first important notion of Eastern spirituality, one which leads to an equanimous vision and a deliverance of the spirit.

22
KILL: ABSOLUTE EVIL?

Tonight, a reader asked me this question: "I read your post on 'The Inseparable Good-Evil'. I would like to ask you if killing is good or bad?"

His trick question implies "what could be the part of the good in a crime?".

I replied: "Even a 10-year-old child, if well educated, knows that killing is bad..

However, do you think all soldiers who go to war think killing is wrong? No, they think they are defending a noble cause (protecting their country from invaders, fighting for freedom, fighting terrorism...) and are in the camp for good.

It is their enemies who are in the camp of evil.

On the other hand, if you are in the other camp,

you will think the opposite. So, in the complexity of human-to-human relationships, the fact of "killing" cannot be clearly described as good or bad, can it? "In fact, it all lies in the intention of the act. If motivated by the shadowless compassion of an ego lurking there, it may even be an honourable act, like killing a dictator like Hitler to save millions in camps. Thus, let us refrain from judging the acts of others, even based on "sure" moral values, accepted by all.

Because it is precisely these value judgments that create discrimination and hatred of the other, often with innocent deaths in ideological battles, when each side gives itself the right to kill, convinced that it is on the right side.

History has shown us this through wars of religion or ideology between humans of different cultures and education. In true spirituality, good and evil are only human concepts, therefore not absolute. In good, there is evil and vice versa. By wanting at all costs to "kill evil" according to his own principles, man ends up "killing the good" which is in him.

Crossing this duality is the first step towards awakening.

23
NEITHER GOOD NOR BAD

Recently, during a class on Eastern spirituality, I tried to explain to my audience the absence of Manichaeism in the Yin-Yang duality, and it seemed to surprise them seriously.

Indeed, we have always been used to reasoning in a Manichean logic: this is beautiful, this is ugly; this is good, this is bad... as if the border which separates them is clear and indisputable.

If this view is reality, the quarrels and divisions among humans and ethical issues would not exist, and courts could be replaced by computers which would easily rule by consulting their pre-established "good-bad" database.

This conceptual view, heavily influenced by religions, creates a kind of morality where anything that does not conform to it becomes "immoral" and bad.

France is currently shaken by the Conflans bombing where a man, believing that a professor had insulted his religion, murdered him. In his view of the facts, it is obvious that he does not think his act is "wrong", quite the contrary.

He thought he was on the "good" side by defending his ideology at the risk of his life.

As long as this duality persists in our way of thinking and acting, we are not close to peace in the world, where quarrels and wars, based mainly on the interests of some to the detriment of others, are endless between the "axis of good" and the "axis of evil".

This dual vision obscures the differences in mentality, culture, education and life histories... It refers to the thinking of some which are opposed to that of others, creating misunderstandings, intolerance, and discrimination. It is only suitable for educating children on their first steps in life as they require limits and social norms. As adults, we need to awaken to true spirituality, with a broader vision and a deeper understanding.

After hours of explanation on the fact that the notions of "good" and "evil" are intimately linked, that those of "evil" must exist for those of "good" to exist (if there is no night, there will be no day either), a participant asked me this question: *"But is it possible that one day, good triumphs and there is no more evil?" Understanding that he was evoking a religious concept, I replied: "In all the sacred texts, when God returns to judge humans on their actions, words and intentions, the good will be rewarded and the bad punished, isn't it? If they are punished, they will go to the dark, away from the light, which means that the darkness, the "evil", will always exist, even when the light, the "good", prevails!"*

This thought plunged him into a moment of doubtful silence, neither good nor bad.

24
THE USURPER OF LOVE

Today, you love a person passionately, as if all your life, your happiness depended on him[4]. One day you realise that he never love you, didn't care for you the way you would have liked, that he had cheated on you... and suddenly your love turns to disgust, hate and pushes you to leave him. There are a lot of people like you, but their love turns to material things, to money, or to their careers... They get bitter when they do not get what they want and feel jealous of those who do get to have them.
What we are used to calling "love" is in fact an

---

4 To increase fluency, the masculine form of all the personal pronouns (he/she), adjectives (his/her), and pronouns (him/her) were used. Of course, when it comes to women, they should their feminine forms.

usurper. It is of the same nature as "hatred". Both are the yin (darkness) and yang (light) sides of the same suffering. Its real name is "attachment". His centre of interest is our "me", our ego: If you love me, I will love you. If you hate me, I will hate you back. I do what is good for me, and avoid what is bad for me, to the detriment of the well-being of others.

"Attachment" is very clever because it has to be able to trick you in order to feed the ego, its child.

He manages to make you believe that you are good and generous, ready to sacrifice yourself for your loved ones, for the poor; that your love is altruistic, transcendent… and you will be so proud that you will continue to make your "me" grow so that it is more and more visible.

Thus, you will continue to suffer from love, to lose yourself between beauty and ugliness, existence and absence, hope and despair, joys and sorrows…

Love is not located at these two ends. It is in the middle, where yin and yang are in perfect balance and neutralise each other. It is the "zero point", Emptiness.

The Void Mind is immense, encompassing everything, from less infinite to more infinite. This love is unsurpassable and inexhaustible. He cannot bring suffering. On the contrary, he will deliver us from "attachment", its usurper, omnipresent in our sleeping minds.

However, our human condition does not allow us to live without a minimum of attachment. The main thing is not to let it become an indispensable condition for our happiness.

25
"DETACHMENT" IS NOT THE CURE FOR "ATTACHMENT"

The ordinary mind or the "attachment mind" works like a camera. When he has captured the image of a person or event, he sees it as a snapshot that will never change.

Taking the photo of a moment of happiness, he forgets that unhappiness could arise after a while.

Taking the photo of a face, of a character trait, he is amazed at how much he has changed after years of no contact. Recalling the good memories of yesteryear, it is sad to see that everything has changed, that the past can never return. And he is in pain.

The "attachment" spirit is constantly tormented, sorry, embittered by its past and anxious about its future. He seeks deliverance by taking many beautiful photos to fill his void, and create points of attachment to deal with unfavourable situations.

When he has had enough with the world around

him, filled with judges, traitors, bad people... he arrives at the "detachment" solution.

The "detachment mind" is also a camera, but the lens is closed with a cap. He found a temporary and superficial peace by remaining deaf to the criticisms and slander of others, blind to the acts which would have revolted him in normal times. He does not care about anything. Since everyone is in the same boat as him, he no longer pays attention to those who arrive or who cannot make it.

In fact, the peace of the "detachment mind" is fleeting. When the "me" is still big, there are things left that it cannot be detached from. He claims the presence of others around him, like planets around the sun. He may also become insensitive to the suffering of others and their need for help.

The "non-attachment mind" sits in the middle of these two extremes. He is like a mirror reflecting things as they are, constantly equanimous, without "good or bad" judgement. He always considers the needs of those around him without demanding a return. However, unlike a camera, when an event has passed, it keeps no images, letting its emotions dissolve. This spirit constantly lives in the present, "here and now," without resentment for the past or anxiety for the future. It is the spirit of deliverance.

26
THE FAKE-REAL AND THE REAL-FAKE SANTA CLAUS

When we see Santa Claus walking through the galleries of a supermarket distributing treats to passers-by, the child in us has the reflex to think that he is a fake Santa Claus. Indeed, he is sometimes too thin, too young to be true and his fake beard is often poorly put on.

The real Santa Claus lives at the North Pole, surrounded by his elves and reindeer.

To be honest, this thought had already crossed my mind at some point, followed by a sudden "awakening": the real-fake Santa Claus (the one in the supermarket) and the fake-real Santa Claus (the one of our imagination) are both fake. Therefore, they are not different in nature.

If we take a deeper look at global or social

conflicts, we will see that the discord always revolves around claims that are considered "real" for some and "fake" for others. The current fashion is to spread fake news via social media to manipulate public opinion. By force, we no longer really distinguish the real from the fake. And yet, we continue to forge certainties about uncertainty and fight for the pseudo-truths that just represent our innermost convictions. So, the world is suffering.

The reality is that there is always something fake in real and real in fake. It all depends on which side we put our egotistical vision to consider.

Therefore, why not look beyond what is right or wrong?

On this Christmas day, isn't the symbolism of Santa Claus the highlighting of the innocence of childhood, where magic is still present, where confidence in what is impossible is still there, is it not the spirit of giving and sharing with all, a little joy and warmth in the cold of winter?

Let us look deep inside: the real-real Santa Claus (or the fake-fake, both being the same) is still here.

He invites us to open our doors for more generosity, brotherhood, friendship and sharing.

For the reward, he will offer our inner child a beautiful Christmas filled with joys and peace, gifts of inestimable value.

27
GOOD ALTERNATIVE MEDICINE

When we talk about alternative medicine, we immediately think of "soft medicine", with therapeutic methods such as herbal medicine, homoeopathy, or acupuncture, supposed to cure us without causing too many side effects.

However, treatment is only part of medicine.

In this regard, I avoid talking about "soft medicine", as opposed to "hard medicine" which heals with chemical drugs and techniques such as surgery or radiotherapy. I prefer to speak of "right medicine", which must begin with an exact diagnostic process, followed by treatment adapted to the disease, whether "soft" or "hard". Indeed, a so-called "soft" medicine can be seriously harmful if it is not adapted to a serious illness, whereas a so-called "hard" medicine can save without creating secondary concerns.

For this reason, although medicine is a science, it is also an art, in which two plus two does not necessarily make four, as other factors may come into play, such as the patient's background (age, sex, previous illnesses, general condition...), lifestyle and mentality.

Today I am going to share with you my concept of "good soft medicine". First, I would like you to forget the "treatment" side of medicine so that it can become holistic again, that it must be interested in the individual as a whole, especially in his mode of life when still in apparent good health.

First, "good soft medicine" is medicine "gentle with oneself". Here are its golden rules:

1. **Love your body**

I sometimes hear during consultations, patients who use harsh words to describe their appearance, such as "I hate my body", "I do not love myself", and "I hate to look at myself in the mirror" because they find themselves "too big". They torture their body with severe restrictive diets, followed by periods of bulimia. This is called the "yoyo phenomenon", encouraged by women's magazines that follow the rhythms of the seasons: eat well during the holidays, lose weight quickly before summer.

If this is the case, my first piece of advice is to relearn how to love and respect your body. If you really love him, you are going to take care of him and he will give it back to you. Take pleasure in eating and never feel guilty. A good meal releases the "feel-good hormone" serotonin, which is good for your morale. However, pay attention to the quality of the food (favour fish, fruits, and seasonal vegetables) as well as the quantity consumed, because your body should not be considered as a "catch-all" where you put anything, in any amount, just to fill it.

Loving your body also means not harming it. Do not give him toxic substances, such as tobacco, alcohol without moderation, or drugs. They will take many years and your quality of life away from you as you get older.

Your body also needs daily exercise. Half an hour of walking or an equivalent effort will suffice. Excessive sport, especially at a high level with competitions, is often bad for your joints and muscles. It will age you faster instead of maintaining your health and youth.

2. **Live in harmony with the seasons**

Oriental medicine considers any living organism as a microcosm that should follow the same laws as the universe, the macrocosm. These rules follow two fundamental principles: Yin (feminine principle) and Yang (masculine principle). Movement, light, heat, exterior, anger, joy... are Yang. Rest, darkness, cold, inside, sadness... are Yin. These two principles are complementary and inseparable (if there is no night, there will be no day) and are constantly changing (nights and days follow one another, as well as the seasons).

In spring, the light gradually replaces the greyness of winter, it is the "little Yang". Insects and animals come out of hibernation. We must also very gradually increase our activities (outings in nature, gentle physical exercises: stretching gently, loosening up, relaxing the back and "open" the chest) and continue to protect ourselves from the spring wind without revealing ourselves too much.

In summer, the sky is very bright, and the temperature rises. This is the "great Yang". Nature is on the move: insects abound, animals come out of their dens, vegetation is lush. Now is the time to get out and live to the fullest with family and friends, but not forgetting to protect yourself from the sun with a hat and sunscreen. Hydrate regularly. Remember, however, to be gentle on your heart and to avoid spikes in blood pressure through excessive or inappropriate exertion.

In autumn ("little Yin") then in winter ("great Yin"), the sky is grey, not very bright, the temperature drops, nature gradually falls asleep: insects hide, animals hibernate, trees lose their foliage. The morale of the human being follows the Yin energy and "goes inside". He must rest like all other living beings, to be able to "come out" stronger next spring. So, if you are feeling a little sad during these seasons, do not be worried. Cut down on your activities and get as much rest as possible, warm indoors with your loved ones. Recharge your batteries for the next cycle of the four seasons.

If you must go out, remember to protect your neck and chest from the cold.

For your diet, fruits, vegetables, and seasonal products are recommended, especially those rich in antioxidants, useful for the prevention of cancer and cardiovascular disease.

Living in harmony with the laws of nature is a habit of life that preserves longevity and well-being.

3. **Take care of your mind**

In his book "The Little Prince", St Exupéry wrote: *"And the truth was that there were some terrible seeds on the planet of the little prince. These were the seeds of baobabs. The soil of the planet was full of them. If you recognize a baobab too late, you will never be able to get rid of it. It spreads over the entire planet. Its roots go right through it. And if the planet is too small, and if the baobabs are too many, they tear the planet apart.*

"It's a question of discipline," the little prince later told me. "When you finish washing and dressing each morning, then it's time to clean your planet very carefully. It's necessary to pull up the baobabs regularly, as soon as you can recognize them. Sometimes it isn't easy because they are similar to roses when they are very young. It's a very boring job, but very easy."

Indeed, our mind is our planet. Our well-being depends on its maintenance. Therefore, remember to regularly pull out the baobab seeds as soon as you notice them (pessimistic thoughts, resentments, hatred, anger, anxiety, irritability...) and never let them take hold of your consciousness.

Practise conscious breathing as soon as you think about it (inflate the abdomen while inhaling, deflate it while exhaling while paying attention to these movements). If you can, do a small meditation session (just sit and breathe) for 15 minutes each night before bed to calm the mind, let go of the tensions of the day and thus increase the quality of sleep.

In addition, a "good soft medicine" is also a medicine "soft with the others". We all know that emotions that are too strong, and not evacuated, can over time injure the body and create disease. Also, let us avoid creating suffering for others with harsh, violent, and hurtful words. Let us get used to nonviolent communication, delicacy, even in frankness and claims.

Children's minds are fragile, but they are the foundations of their happiness as adults. Let us give them gentleness in words and actions, self-confidence in encouragement and a favourable environment so that they can grow up in good physical and psychological health.

In conclusion, good alternative medicine brings fulfilment and well-being to the body and mind despite the inevitable onset of old age and illnesses.

It also aims to establish harmonious human-to-human relations, thus avoiding creating unnecessary suffering, sources of imbalances and illnesses.

28
SMILE AT LEAST ONCE AN HOUR!

One evening, I received an 88-year-old granny for consultation. Her face does not express happiness. Her wrinkles seem to mark a suffering past.

She told me of having lived her childhood during the Second World War, where the fear of the bombings installed in her a permanent insecurity to this day.

"And yet," she told me, "I *have everything I need to be happy: I have four children and seven adorable grandchildren who surround me every day, affection. I do not miss anything, but I still feel sad and unhappy. What medicine will you give me, doctor?"*

"Here is your prescription, ma'am: smile at least once an hour, every day, except when you are asleep!"

She looks at me with her eyes wide with astonishment: *"Is it true that I will be better?"*

His accompanying granddaughter understood my intention. She said to her grandmother, "Start smiling now, grandma!"

And the old lady gives me a big smile. She was so beautiful and radiant as if her past was forgotten for a magical moment.

In traditional Chinese medicine, a smile translates to the joy of the Fire movement, which is linked to the Heart. It opens the door to transcendent happiness because the Heart shelters the Spirit which communicates with the top.

"Don't forget to smile at least once an hour, Grandma, and see you in a month, you'll hear from you!".

Whatever the outcome, the seed of joy was sown.

29
MEDITATION: DO NOT LOOK FOR WELL-BEING AT ALL COSTS!

Zen Buddhism meditation came to the West in the 1970s, first with Transcendental Meditation, then with the Mindfulness-Based Stress Reduction (MBSR) program developed by the biologist Jon Kabat-Zinn.

The latter has secularised his nature to adapt it to Westerners, who are in a constant search for happiness and improvement in their performance.

As a result, meditation loses its spiritual nature and enters an ordinary vision of seeking well-being through appeasement of the mind, forgetting its deep purpose which is the understanding of the root of the suffering of the mind, the only path leading to unalterable inner peace.

The West was awakened sharply when recent

studies revealed side effects of meditation, especially in people who practise it intensely. We describe states of euphoria or intense physical pain, visions, anger, and fear, even paranoia.

These symptoms are known from Buddhist accounts and are considered to be signs of the meditator's progress.

Simply put, the original meditation has two phases: Samatha (mental stillness) and Vipassana (insight). Imagine the mind like a glass of muddy water. During the Samatha phase, keeping the mind still and paying attention to the breath causes the mud to settle on the bottom of the glass and the water becomes transparent again. The work of Vipassana consists, with a clear mind, in observing the body, its sensations and perceptions, and analysing their impermanence and their nature. This work leads over time to a correct understanding of the non-self. This is the process of filtering the sludge that remains on the bottom of the glass.

In this phase, all the resentments and pains buried in the subconscious or masked by a hectic daily life can resurface and lead to a feeling of ill-being during meditation. Eastern spirituality guides the meditator therefore towards the practice of the equanimous, non-discriminating mind. It consists of observing the pleasant or unpleasant sensations that arise in our body and mind by putting ourselves in the position of an outside observer, without any judgement.

Let us let go in times of calm as well as in times of restlessness and pain. The sensations will disappear by their impermanence.

The practice of meditation can continue in our daily lives trying to always keep the mind equanimous: "I do not systematically seek the feeling of well-being, nor reject that of unhappiness every moment of my day. I accept it as it is".

This equanimous spirit is the Zen spirit, the spirit of the Insite: "things are just like this".

The more we train ourselves to be equanimous in all circumstances, the more easily we will weather the storms of this hectic life full of the unexpected.

30
THE INFINITE COMPLEXITY OF THE CAUSALITY

You have surely seen a video of a "mad" inventor (I wish I had his madness 😊) who develops a machine where every action triggers another action, like the fall of one domino and the fall of another. Thus, while eating his soup, he pulls on a string, which overturns a flower pot falling on a hammer which strikes a lever which then raises a bucket... Let us suppose that this "machine" comprises a series of a thousand actions and that in the 120th action, the door of a cage opens allowing a bird to escape, the unfurling of its wings triggering the 121st action. We can hardly guess that the bird was able to get out of its cage because this man had eaten his soup, time before!

In 1972, Edward Lorenz at a scientific conference amazed the audience with the following question:

"Predictability: Does the flap of a butterfly's wings in Brazil set off a tornado in Texas?"

Indeed, in nature, the multiplicity of factors that can act on an event is infinitely large that any slight action could trigger a phenomenon without common measure, provided it is performed at the right time, when all the factors are in place to allow this to happen.

Let us come back to man and his mind, the area that interests us.

When I was an intern, while on duty in the emergency room, I was often surprised by the suicides of young adults following a simple sentimental disappointment. I then decided to make it my thesis subject to better understand the cause. I then discovered the complexity of the human mind in the face of events it had experienced since childhood. Sentimental disappointment is just the straw that broke the camel's back, filled with resentments, disappointments, and frustrations, not emptied, or cleaned up since childhood.

Often in my consultations, I hear suffering patients ask me the question to which I have no answer: "Why?", as:

- Why are my colleagues so mean to me?

- Why do all these injustices happen to me alone?

- Why did he cheat on me, let me down despite everything I have done for him?

- Why do I have this cancer when I have a healthy life?

- Why do I have this autoimmune disease that is killing my life?...

All I can tell them is that something has happened

at a specific time in their life, for example an unfortunate word at the wrong time, a conflict settled in too violent communication, an action that triggers suffering in others. Negative emotions reinforced by the energy of habit leading to hatred of others, hating one's own image with feelings of guilt... so many factors so complex to analyse that the only answer that seems to me to be correct is: "things are just that way ".

In Eastern spirituality, we call this "karma", the continuation of a long chain of cause and effect. What differentiates it from "destiny" is the fact that we are also actors and not only spectators of our destiny. Thus, we can act on our future, by properly rearranging our present.

Let us do like Norbert, the chef who challenges himself to make a gourmet dish from what we have in your fridge, without asking why we only have these ingredients and nothing else. He just uses what he has on hand and always wins his bet.

So, let us transform our lives by choosing to press the right button or operate the right lever. How would we know it is the right one? It is quite simple, just read the labels below. If we see words like "love", "compassion", "non-violence", "peace", and "letting go"..., we risk absolutely nothing.

I am sure that these butterfly wing beats will cause tornadoes of happiness in our lives.

31
ALL IN ONE

In ancient times, the Emperor of China summoned a famous painter from the kingdom who lived secluded from the world in a cave on the mountain, to ask him to paint a dragon on the wall of the royal library.

He wished this dragon was not mundane like any other dragon made to date. The painter asked to give him time to study the matter.

Months passed and still no news from the painter.

Each emissary sent by the king to the cave where the latter lives received the same response: "Please tell his Majesty that I still need time to realise his dragon".

Finally, the big day arrived. The painter bowed down to the king and then stood in front of the great white wall of the royal library. Lifting his heavy brush with one hand, he completed his work in one stroke in less than a minute. The king was amazed because he expected a long and painstaking job after all these months of waiting and had the painter executed for contempt.

During the weeks which followed the death of the latter, the king tormented himself day and night. While trying to understand his gesture, he went to the cave where the painter lived. As soon as he walked through the entrance, the king saw on the stone walls two magnificent dragons in flaming colours and he thought in amazement, "Why didn't you paint these dragons for me? I would have covered you with gold!".

The further he walked into the cave, the more simplified the dragons on the walls were: fewer and fewer colours, fewer and fewer details. Arriving at the painter's bed, the king saw a dragon painted with a single stroke, like the one painted on the wall of the royal library. He sat on the bed and stared at the painting. This dragon seemed to him alive, looked at him with piercing eyes and moved according to the rays of light which entered the cave. And he suddenly realised that it was a masterpiece, far above any dragons he had seen before.

Thus, the wise men who dedicate their lives to their spiritual quest reduce their teachings to very few words, even to silence if necessary.

The Zen expression, "the overwhelming silence", shook me when I finally understood it.

Illumination burst like lightning, followed by deafening thunder, in the silence of meditation.

Do not look for it in heaven.

Neither outside. Nor inside.

32
THE IMPORTANCE OF "ZERO POINT"

Our mind is like a scale. Theoretically, when in a neutral state (neither joy nor sorrow), the needle should be at the zero point. When he is satisfied, and happy, the needle tilts on the positive side. When frustrated and sad, the needle tilts on the negative side. However, by enduring the emotional storms of our daily lives without a minimum of adjustment, our scales are out of order and often remain stuck elsewhere than at zero point.

What if it hangs on the positive side?

Our mind is like a child without candy who is given one every day. Its zero-point is "zero candy". So he's happy when he gets one, because "a candy" = +1, so his scales are tipping on the positive side.

Imagine this child receiving two candies each day. If one day he only gets one, he will be unhappy. Why? Because his zero point was "two candies", therefore "one candy" = -1, which tilts his balance on the negative side!

One day, I was walking past a gadget store that was selling off all its stock at -50% before it closed. People jostled each other, emptied shelves, and filled their caddies with unnecessary items, just because the lust was kindled by a frantic urge for possession.

This "positive side" has a name, Greed. The greed-nurtured mind is insatiable no matter what the condition of its life. We are all amazed to see multimillionaires arrested for tax evasion when what they have is enough to support them for many lifetimes. In fact, their "zero point" is so out of the way of the hundreds of millions that losing a few dozen seems unbearable to them, to the point of taking the risk of losing everything and falling into pain.

However, it is not just others who are greedy. We just must look deep inside to see that the needle of our scale is also stuck on the "plus" side, always more, more, more...

What if it hangs on the negative side?

I see a lot of patients who are still struggling with their past as if the suffering they had gone through was preventing them from ever achieving happiness. They like to rehash and analyse their childhood, adolescence, problems, and conflicts, again and again. Their scale needle is stuck at -100, so they are unable to take advantage of the +10, +20, even +90... moments that come in their life, as the total score will always remain negative.

This "negative side" has a name, Ignorance. The mind is totally dedicated to the service of the ego and lives curled up on itself.

Thus, awakening mind training is about constantly returning to "zero point" (or primary point), whether the emotion is positive or negative. The more frequently you return to your "zero point", the more serene your life will be.

"A mind that oscillates little in a constantly moving world" is one of the keys to happiness.

33
AROUND THE CORN LEAVES

Mrs A. was angry. Her land adjoins that of a farmer "thrifty up to 50 cm of soil" who planted his maize close to his fence. "And every year, when he cuts his corn, a thick carpet of leaves falls on my land," she told me with her eyes filled with anger.

"I walked over to my fence and I assure you he heard everything on my mind!".

And she had a lot of it: irritability, sleep disturbances, headaches…

"If you changed your mind and thought that every year, he gave you compost for free, in large quantities and delivered to your home, wouldn't that be better?"

"It's true, but it's not organically grown!"

"And yet, we continue to eat our corn without any

problem, so its leaves must not be harmful to your soil!"

"Indeed, to think like that... "

"Yes, make peace with your neighbour, you will gain much more! Already peace of mind, sleep, and health.

One day, bring him a dish that you have cooked".

"I just baked lots of cakes to give to my neighbours for the holidays!"

"But not for him?"

"No, not for him!"

"Get him some cakes, I'm sure that's a lot more effective than screaming. Make peace with your neighbour ".

We had a good laugh at this last consultation of the year, around corn husks.

Each event always has two sides, bright (Yang) and dark (Yin). We often tend to emphasise their darkness and clutter our minds with resentments, anger, and frustration.

Let us try, in the face of an unfortunate event in our lives, to look for its luminous side and we will see that luck will smile on us at every moment.

34
A FRIENDLY WORLD

The first time I read this book, I really did not understand why St Exupéry had landed the Little Prince in an arid, depopulated desert when he arrived on planet Earth.

He could only converse with a serpent and "a flower of nothing at all," when the Earth had such large cities populated by people, much more joyful and likeable. Here is this passage:

"Earth is not just any planet! There are one hundred and eleven kings, seven thousand geographers, nine hundred thousand businessmen, seven and a half million drunks, three hundred and eleven million conceited, that is to say about two billion grown-ups. [...]

The little prince, once on earth, was therefore very surprised not to see anyone. [...]

- Where are the men? finally resumed the little prince. We are a little alone in the desert...

- We are also alone among men, said the snake.

The little prince crossed the desert and met with only one flower. It was a flower with three petals, a flower of no account at all.

"Good morning," said the little prince.

"Good morning," said the flower.

"Where are the men?" the little prince asked, politely.

The flower had once seen a caravan passing.

"Men?" she echoed. "I think there are six or seven of them in existence. I saw them, several years ago. But one never knows where to find them. The wind blows them away. They have no roots, and that makes their life very difficult".

"Goodbye," said the little prince.

"Goodbye," said the flower.. [...]

The little prince climbed a high mountain. The only mountains he had ever known were the three volcanoes, which came up to his knees. And he used the extinct volcano as a footstool. "From a mountain as high as this one," he said to himself, "I shall be able to see the whole planet at one glance, and all the people...". But he saw nothing, save peaks of rock that were sharpened like needles.

"Good morning," he said courteously.

"Good morning--Good morning--Good morning," answered the echo.

"Who are you?" said the little prince.

"Who are you--Who are you--Who are you?" answered the echo.

"Be my friends. I am all alone," he said.

"I am all alone--all alone--all alone," answered the echo.

"What a queer planet!" he thought. "It is altogether dry, and altogether pointed, and altogether harsh and forbidding. And the people have no imagination. They repeat whatever one says to them... On my planet I had a flower; she always was the first to speak..."[5]

There are two worlds: the "just like this" world with its joys and sorrows and the world "as we perceive it", which changes according to our emotions. When we are happy, the world seems like a rare jewel, of such beauty that makes us vibrate. When we are anxious, sad, or afraid, it will appear threatening, deserted, or sick.

Fear is the worst emotion. When we are afraid, we become suspicious of others. We question their sincerity as if gratuitous kindness is always questionable unless the person is naive or foolish and does not know what they're really doing.

With fear in our stomachs, we behave like *"the donkey dressed in the skin of the lion"* from La Fontaine's fable to scare others. We want to show

---

5   Extracts from the book "The Little Prince" by St Exupéry

them that we have no fear and are ready to go to war, until the end, to fight any injustice committed against us.

This "lion skin" is not us. It is just a mask that makes us believe that we are strong and makes us forget for a moment our lack of self-confidence, our fear of the gaze and judgments of others.

It is our ego, which ceaselessly demands attention, respect, fidelity, loyalty, truth, justice... but which remains hungry despite everything because the world we live in does not seem ready to change for us, and we suffer.

In addition, the wars and conflicts that we have created with those around us often leave disastrous consequences for our future. We sowed the wind, but we are afraid to reap the storm. The world then seems more and more threatening to us.

If this is the case, my first advice is to "lay down your arms" and take off your "bulletproof vest". Wars increase violence, leave indelible scars, fuel hatred and fear. A world without weapons, without violence, may at first glance seem dangerous to you, even utopian. And yet, experiment by yourself for a few months: do not hurt anyone anymore, not in words, not in actions, even in thoughts.

Melt your ego, become downright naive, accept wrongs, and change your behaviour by putting compassion forward. You will see how happy it is to live in a friendly world, dancing with wolves and swimming with sharks.

I am going to end this chapter of the desert with a sentence addressed by the Little Prince to St Exupéry on leaving the earth to return to his planet: *"And at night you will look up at the stars. It's too small, where I live, for me to show you where my star is. It is better that way. My star will just be one of the stars, for you. So you'll like looking at all of them. They will all be your friends."*.

And our world will become a friendly world!

35
WHAT ARE WE LOOKING FOR?

Here is a passage from St Exupéry's "The Little Prince" that many people ignore:

"Good morning," said the little prince.

"Good morning," said the railway switchman.

"What is it that you do here?" asked the little prince.

"I sort the travellers into bundles of a thousand," the switchman said. "I dispatch the trains that carry them, sometimes to the right, sometimes to the left."

And a brightly lit express train, roaring like thunder, shook the switchman's cabin.

"What a hurry they're in," said the little prince. "What are they looking for?"

"Not even the engineer on the locomotive knows,"

the switchman said.

And another brightly lit express train thundered by in the opposite direction.

"Are they coming back already?" asked the little prince.

"They're not the same ones," the switchman said. "It's an exchange."

"They weren't satisfied, were they?" asked the little prince.

"No one is ever satisfied where he is," the switchman said.

This passage illustrates well the great distress of our time. We live "keeping our noses to the grindstone" and have accumulated a lot of material goods in our life, achieved several goals of youth. And yet, we are not satisfied with our conditions. Worse, we do not even know what we want to be good about ourselves, to be happy.

Happiness seems to be in the camp of the rich, who have no material concerns and have a comfort of life enviable by all. However, we know that money does not protect them from sentimental problems, family conflicts, legal troubles... It can even lead many people to immense losses.

Happiness also seems to be in the camp of movie or song stars, television stars, who are adored, respected, and followed by millions of people. Yet many of them are overwhelmed by sadness and depression. Some will even kill themselves or drown in alcohol and drugs.

If happiness is neither in wealth nor in fame, then would it be in the family? In children? In love? In health? The answer seems difficult: families can separate, children can be the cause of a lot of worries, love can be followed by betrayal and abandonment, health is never perfect...

We can continue to search, starting in all directions, like the trains in the story of The Little Prince.

One day, we will end up asking this fundamental question for our life: does happiness really exist outside of fleeting moments of joy?

Everything passes, all weary.

Only our original nature is immutable and eternal. You do not have to look everywhere else. We are the happiness.

When our mind is connected with our "Great-Self" (or "Great-All"), we are in fullness. Love and happiness are our ultimate nature. We are billionaires and need nothing more than what life has in store for us. We fully live every moment of our life.

The problem is our ego, the "Little-Self" who believes himself to be poor and thus spends his life insatiably filling his emptiness: money, power, fame, pleasure, respect, feeling, justice... for himself. The more we have, the more our need grows. It is as if we are drinking seawater to quench our thirst.

Being happy is not that hard. You just have to wake up, rise up, get out of the borders of selfishness and make the right choices.

36
A TIME FOR EVERY STEP

Give ourselves

A time to work, a time to rest,

A time for material goods, a time for spiritual wellbeing,

A time to worry, a time to surrender,

A time to cry, a time to heal,

A time to talk, a time to meditate,

A time to reach out to others, a time to come back to oneself,

A time to practise, a time to have fun,

A time to think, a time to let go,

A time to believe, a time to seek to understand for yourself,

A time to follow the rules, a time to invent them,
A time to teach, a time to learn,
A time to fight and a time to love.

Antoine de St Exupéry's fox taught the Little Prince: "It's the time you lost for your rose that makes your rose so important".
Also, give ourselves
A time to tame and a time to be tamed.

However, let us not hurry!
Let us give time to time...

37
THE GATELESS BARRIER

One of the most famous Zen books is called "The Gateless Barrier" (Wu Men Guan 無門 關).

It is a collection of 48 zen koans compiled, published in 1228 by the Chinese monk Wu Men (無門) (1183-1260).

A koan is often an absurd question or a story of conversation between two Zen masters, completely meaningless to the uninitiated person.

Each koan is a key that opens a door to enlightenment on a higher and higher level.

However, although each of them is a barrier not closed by a door, few can pass through it.

It is as if travellers from all walks of life stop at a warning sign: "Anyone who wants to cross this passage must leave all their luggage: knowledge, opinion, prejudices, conceptual vision and may even lose their life!".

Many of us hope for a major life change or even a total renewal. That said, we must change our way of thinking and seeing things, to analyse events in a neutral and equanimous way, we often refuse to quit our habits, often taking refuge behind all our conditioning since childhood: education. , mentality, religion, tradition...

Therefore, although we put a lot of effort into improving our lives and our relationships with others to come out of our suffering, the results often do not live up to our expectations.

Would we be prepared to drop all this bulky baggage here to go through this gate without a gate today?

Zen master Wu Men wrote in the preface to the book:

"T*he Great Way has no door.*

There are a thousand paths leading to it.

Whoever manages to cross this door of Emptiness,

Will walk freely between Heaven and Earth".

38
THE EMPTY AND THE FULL, THE VISIBLE AND THE INVISIBLE (1)

In his work "Physics" in Book IV, Aristotle, a philosopher of Antiquity, denies the existence of a vacuum and asserts its incompatibility with movement. He said that "Nature abhors a vacuum". In this philo-scientific debate of his time, Parmenides, his adversary, thinks that "if the void is nothing, it cannot exist". So if the void exists, it must be full.

Edgard Gunzig, professor of theoretical physics at the Free University of Brussels, and Isabelle Stengers, scientific philosopher, wrote in their book "The vacuum": *"Today the vacuum is different from nothing. He would even be the central actor in the history of matter and the Universe, the privileged partner of physics. Emptiness and matter are no longer two separate manifestations of nature but two aspects of the same reality."*

Six hundred years before our era, Lao Zi, the father of Taoism, had explained in the *"The Book of The Way and its Virtue"* (Dao De Jing):

"Thirty spokes share the hub of a wheel;
yet it is its centre that makes it useful.
You can mould clay into a vessel;
yet, it is its emptiness that makes it useful.
Cut doors and windows from the walls of a house,
the ultimate use of the house
will still depend on that part where nothing exists.
Therefore, something is shaped into what is;
but its usefulness comes from what is not."

Thus, "form / matter" (Yin) and "non-form / void" (Yang) are the two inseparable aspects of the same reality. Their opposition is not manichean. Water in liquid form is visible, so Yin. When it evaporates as a gas, it becomes invisible, so Yang.

Yin descends in the form of rain (formlessness becomes form), and Yang rises in the form of vapour (form becomes formless).

Nothing is lost, nothing is created, and everything is transformed. We are thus witnessing "small deaths" of H_2O, which are, in reality, only its transformations.

The cycle of mutation between Yin and Yang never stops. "Form" is "Non-form" and vice versa.

If we only see the "Form" and not the "Non-form" our vision is not yet subtle.

But if we can see the "Form" in the "Non-form"

and the "Non-form" in the "Form", our vision becomes subtle.

    Take the time to understand this, and you will enter an unsuspected universe, with invaluable life lessons.

39
THE EMPTY AND THE FULL, THE VISIBLE AND THE INVISIBLE (2)

In an article in the science magazine Symmetry, physicist Ali Sendermier gave a great insight into the void of the universe.

Our bodies are made up of billions of atoms. Etymologically, the word "atom" comes from the Greek "atomos" which means "indivisible".

However, since the beginning of the 20th century, several experiments have demonstrated the existence of different particles constituting the atom: protons (positively charged) and neutrons (which are not charged) located in the nucleus, as well as electrons, negatively charged, which revolve around the nucleus and constitute the "electron cloud" of the atom.

There is a void between the nucleus of the atom and its electron cloud, which is 100,000 times larger than it. So if the kernel is the size of a bean, its cloud would be at least as big as a baseball stadium.

If all this void were to disappear, the human body would be reduced to the size of a grain of dust and all of humanity with its 7 billion people would fit in a lump of sugar.

Indeed, all of us, as well as our huge universe, are made up of 99.9999999% void.

At this very moment, our fingers have never touched the computer keyboard and our seat has never supported our gluteal muscles. What we perceive is just the electromagnetic force of repulsion between the different electrons of matter.

If almost everything is empty, how can we weigh 70 kg?

The answer is energetic! Indeed, protons and neutrons are made up of elementary particles, quarks, linked very strongly to each other by gluons. It is this force of attraction that gives mass and visibility to matter.

If we cannot go through walls, it's because emptiness has never been empty! It is filled with energy in the form of waves and invisible magnetic fields. This is how we can see and touch our surroundings.

Advances in quantum physics bring us closer to the basics of Eastern spirituality.

So, what we think we understand with our senses is not really what it is.

We just see a visible illusion created by an arrangement of the invisible, the nature of which, illusory, cannot be permanent. Indeed, the mutation between the visible and the invisible being perpetual by its energetic nature, any material object is in reality only a temporal phenomenon.

    Only a subtle sight can see its true nature, a still and unchanging void, devoid of all concepts. Taoism calls it "Dao". Buddhism calls it "Emptiness".

40
THE EMPTY AND THE FULL, THE VISIBLE AND THE INVISIBLE (3)

When comparing traditional Asian painting (Chinese, Korean, Japanese, and Vietnamese) and Western painting, the detail that strikes the eye is the Void omnipresent in the first and always absent in the second.

This intentional void is of capital importance in the dynamism of Asian painting.

Indeed, it is only "visually empty" but its nature is filled with life energy, Qi, which energises space and time.

It allows the free movement of the gaze of the observer, which is no longer limited within the framework of the work. Thus, when the latter contemplates the unpainted sky, he can "see" it beyond the limits of the painting because his mind goes to distant horizons with his imaginary gaze which extends.

The mutation of everything involves interactions and exchanges with the environment surrounding it. It is in an empty space that these exchanges can take place.

Without it, everything will occupy its defined place in a full space, without any possible dynamism.

The acupuncture point is a beautiful illustration of the energy of the Void in the human body. Its ideogram is 穴 ("Xué") which literally means "Cave".

It is often located near a joint, between the insertion of a tendon in the bone or in a gap between two muscles. Ideally, it does not contain any vessels, nerves, muscles, or tendons. The emptier it is, the more powerful its energy.

Likewise, in human relationships, the distance between individuals allows them to evolve and interact with each other. Without this distance, this space of individual freedom, relationships suffocate and end up breaking down to allow each protagonist to breathe again.

So, let us respect this essential distance in a couple by avoiding mistrust, surveillance, incessant crises of jealousy that stifle love.

If we are parents, let our children have the freedom to think, create and discover new horizons, even if they are beyond our comprehension.

There you go, now you know (almost) everything about the Void. It is not a concept that is opposed to "Full" because it IS full.

This non-opposing view is the basis of the non-dual reality of Eastern spirituality.

The spiritual journey will awaken us to the "non-self", a "void of the self" which does not reduce the self to nothing, on the contrary. The absence of ego will allow everyone to connect to the "Great All", to the original Emptiness, like the waves returning to the ocean. They then realise that they are not just "waves", but entirely "the ocean".

41
THOUGHT GUIDES ENERGY

If you read me regularly, you now know that everything is energy, even matter.

There are subtle energy forms that are often overlooked, such as those of emotions.

Indeed, anger increases our strength tenfold, joy pushes us to reach out to others, sadness makes us prefer isolation and fear paralyses us or gives us strength in our legs to run away.

This energy of emotions is guided by thought. You have surely experienced it more than once: on Sunday, when you wake up, a think of the joy of a day walking with friends makes you jump out of bed. However, just thinking of a tiring day at work waiting for you is enough to tire you out before you start it. Thinking of a loved one is like a ray of sunshine that illuminates the moment and makes your heart shudder. Thinking of a hated individual or an offence arouses anger like a forest fire ready to devour everything in its path.

In Oriental Medicine, we say that it is "the Yi (thought) that guides the Qi (energy)". If the thinking is clear and compassionate, the energy will be positive and benevolent. It nourishes, flourishes and can sometimes heal. If the thought is tormented, hateful and resentful, the energy will be harmful and malicious. It destroys, causes regression, and can cause disease.

So our thoughts are our friends or our enemies, our ailments or our caregivers. We are the first to hurt ourselves, long before those we accuse. We are also the first to take care of ourselves, long before doctors intervene.

In acupuncture classes, I always emphasise the intention to put in every needle you put. The more compassion you put into it, the more effective the puncture will be. This is the best way to "hammer it home, our way back home."

The good energy offered to others is never wasted. She is like the flame of a candle that remains intact after thousands of shares. Do not block your thinking on ego demands (respect or fairness in return, justice or gratitude demanded...). If you lose a few times, you will win a hundred times as much.

Also, let us change our clothes often to our thoughts. Let us dress them up in colour and throw the rags of the past in the trash. Cultivate a thought that is confident in what life has in store for us, optimistic and loving.

You will see that over time even your outward physical appearance will change. He will shine and everyone will notice his transformation. It is the effect of energy on matter.

According to Dao De Jing, *"until the end of his life, [the realised man] is in no danger"*.

42
INNER HARMONY

The human body has extraordinary capacities, including that of maintaining homeostasis. This means that any imbalance immediately results in the establishment of internal regulation to restore physiological balance. He adapts his hormone levels and uses all his available resources to keep his biological constants and his body temperature unchanged. It mobilizes its immune system to protect the body against external invasions (bacteria, viruses, etc.) and its internal enemies, the "mutant" cells that try to escape its control to become cancerous.

One can thus compare the human body to a walled city where the inhabitants live in a certain harmony, with soldiers who watch any disturbance coming from the outside or the inside.

To identify these threats, everything that is

recognized as "self" or "pro-self" is preserved. On the other hand, everything that is recognized as "anti-self" is neutralised.

However, this wonderful machine can go off the rails and view the "self" as the enemy. This is the case with autoimmune diseases in which the body develops autoantibodies against its own constituents (glands, muscles, cell nuclei, DNA, etc.).
On the other hand, it can tolerate "anti-self" as well as "mutant" cells, allowing them to develop into cancerous diseases without eliminating them.

In addition, there are also conditions called "auto-inflammatory", in which the joints or intestines "become inflamed" for no apparent reason.

If medicine knows perfectly well these diseases, their evolution, and their treatments, it is still ignorant as to their origins.

Here is a text taken from a reference book of traditional Chinese medicine, the origin of which dated back more than 3000 years, the "Classic of the Yellow Emperor - The Essential Questions": *"the Sages of Antiquity learned, by calm and concentration, to maintain their natural energy in docility, to contain their minds well within so that illnesses are taken without hold. Thanks to the restriction of appetites and the containment of inclinations, the heart remains peaceful and unmoved, the body works without exhausting itself, the energy follows a regular course and each of them is satisfied. Appreciating their food, content with their clothes, merry in their mediocrity, without envy for higher conditions, people were what one calls "simple". No greed tarnished their gaze, no disturbance reached their hearts for they were conforming to the Dao. They reached a hundred years of age without their activity tiring because their virtue was unfailing ".*

Of course, this text belongs to the era when science did not yet exist. It does not, therefore, have the vocation to prove any origin of such or such disease, nor to deny the progress of modern medicine.

It just emphasises the importance of our inner harmony on our health.

When the "self" or the ego does not need to fight against its enemies and has no boundaries with others, emotions are soothed, thoughts are fluid and energy flows without hindrance or stagnation. Therefore, apart from constitutional factors or a hostile environment, our body will not leave any favourable ground for the development of these "self-destructive" diseases.

43
IN SUMMARY, WHAT IS OUR LIFE?

Our life is like a ball of dough.

We can make a lot of rolls out of it or a nice brioche if we put butter (and even a few chocolate chips), a pie shell or beautiful cakes...

With imagination and a little salt, we can create all kinds of dreams.

However, we must roll up our sleeves, get our hands dirty, take the courage to get up early, redo the failed batches and keep the soul of a child to constantly create new things.

In short, our life is our work, resulting from our choices and not from those of destiny.

Karma causes that when the croissants are made, friends arrive for breakfast, but not before!

44
LIKE A FLOWER ON WATER

Imagine that we are a flower floating on the surface of a river, carried away by the current, over the years, from one place to another, never turning back.

There are times when the stream is peaceful. The sun warms and blossoms us, butterflies and dragonflies dance with us. Everything is fine.

There are also perilous crossings of the waterfalls with a lot of turbulence, days of rain, or storm falling heavily on us. Everything is going wrong.

Our mind filters all these events and keeps some of them according to our mental disposition.

If we are optimistic, happy times will serve as an engine for us to move forward in life happily.

Unhappy moments will become life lessons, experiences that help us grow in spirituality.

If we are pessimistic, the happy moments will quickly be forgotten, giving way to a series of bad luck episodes in which we will be perpetual victims. After a long period of suffering, some might see life as nonsense and lose all zest for life.

In short, life is never, and for anyone, "a long quiet river". If some people seem to be happier than others, it is just because they made the right choice to be happy no matter what their life circumstances are.

Let us go back to the image of the flower floating on a stream. We can learn a lot from this.

First, the past is already behind us. We will not be able to come back to change anything. As beautiful as it is, this past is already far behind. Regrets will only increase our pain.

Agreeing to turn the page and no longer look to the past will free us from a heavy burden that darkens our present.

Sometimes we regret not having made a dam to divert the stream in another direction that seemed more favourable to us, thus making our future better. Nothing is less sure!

By manipulating our world, we can create unforeseeable consequences far worse than if we had allowed the natural to unfold without a hitch.

When the river bends, we cannot guess what lies ahead behind the bend.

This is where our spirituality will come in. If you are a believer, surrender yourself to providence, "thy will be done". If you are in the mainstream of Eastern spirituality, trust the "natural" (Taoism) or "karma" (Buddhism) which will always choose the best path for you, at this precise moment.

Whatever our choice, let us keep our confidence in the life that continues to flow with its joys and sorrows, its moments of serenity and suffering.

Let us not resist. Let his current carry us away and gradually discover his image when the different pieces of his puzzle are completed. It will become more clear and more understandable day by day.

It is the image of the meaning of our life, here and now, always, and forever.

45
START AWAY FROM EVERYTHING

Who among us had never dreamed of going far, far away, leaving behind all the weight of family, professional, and personal conflicts to be alone on a desert island or in a place unknown until then? , with the hope of starting all over again?

There are multiple reasons for this dream. The most common is sentimental disappointment. We would like to go far away to forget or to hope that the other can suffer the weight of our absence. In the 90s, the boy band "2 be 3" sang:

"To leave a day without return, to erase our love, without looking back, Not to regret, to keep the moments that we have stolen. Leave one day, without luggage, forget your image, without looking back, Not to regret, to think about tomorrow, to start again".

It is also the hope of finding a moment of respite where we can finally drop the burden that has weighed on our shoulders for too long: pressures, stress, toxic relationships…

Imagine that this dream is realised and that we find ourselves alone on our island, we would see that our problems will not be solved at all. Indeed, in our mental baggage, we will surely bring all our sufferings and their alleged perpetrators. They will accompany us every moment, to every corner of our dream beach and will transform it into a nightmarish place.

We will find that there is no point in going far. Whatever we do, our prison will follow us and continue to hinder our true deliverance.

We often forget that life is a long road where at every crossroads we must make a choice to go in one direction or another. We often make the wrong choice out of attachment, tradition, upbringing, fear of the unknown, fear of having to step out of our comfort zone and find ourselves alone. Above all, we find it exceedingly difficult to recognize our mistakes and have the courage to rectify them.

However, if you still want to go extremely far and find peace of mind, I know a good travel agency that will help you find your dream destination.

Sit down. Close your eyes. Breathe in slowly and deeply as you inflate your stomach, then breathe out fully as you retract your abdominal muscles to better force air out of your lungs.

Slowly, you will see your island appear from your window, green, calm, and serene.

Here, there is no loneliness, but a permanent connection with an immense universal love that nothing and no one can dry up.

"Passengers bound for Universe are urged to proceed to the Stargate for imminent departure!" «.

Have a nice trip!

46
PLAN EVERYTHING

When I was a young intern, an anaesthetist invited us for a "farewell drink" before his retirement. He told us that he had everything planned to live happy days with his wife, whom he had not seen much during his years at work. He had built a nice house with a pool that he had not really taken advantage of. He was already planning a trip around the world to celebrate his new freedom. He dreamed of riding his bike every day and having fun with his grandchildren.

Sadly, I learned that he died a week later from a severe brain haemorrhage. It was the only thing he had forgotten to plan.

Most of us live with this forgetfulness, especially when we are still young. We forget that our present existence could end any time, and that we can suddenly lose a loved one, left low on the scale of our priorities.

We also forget that we will not be able to take anything with us when the time to leave comes and that the only things of value we leave are the fond memories and marks of love that we have planted in our lives.

Whether we are right or wrong in conflicts, what could we still hope to gain, if our hearts are heavy with resentment before parting forever?

It is probably time for us to plan the basics before we leave or say goodbye. That moment could be tonight, a few days, a few months, or a few years from now.

It does not matter. The main thing Is to be always ready.

Also, I invite you to make these preparations, the baggage of which could be heavy for some but essential: present your sincere apologies to those you have hurt, forgive those who have hurt you, come to terms, repair the damage you have caused, give attention, affection, love, compassion to others...

Imagine the peace of mind when the bags are packed well before the departure time.

47
DURATION AND FLIGHT PLAN

If we compare our lifespan to that of a flight in an aeroplane, birth would correspond to take-off and death to landing.

The duration of the flight is dependent on the quantity of gasoline taken for take-off, so we are not equal when it comes to longevity. Some of us have a large reservoir predisposing to a long life, others have one of more limited capacity, allowing only a short trip in this world.

To extend this stay, we have several solutions within our reach: choose a healthy and moderate diet, do not bring toxins into the body (tobacco, alcohol, drugs, etc.), perform regular physical exercises...

However, an American study published in August 2019 in the journal *Proceedings of the National Academy of Sciences* (PNAS) showed that the main factor of longevity is optimism!

Indeed, optimistic men live 11% longer than pessimists, and in women, longevity is increased by 15%. According to the authors, the mechanism that would explain the effect of optimism on longevity is that *"Optimists have a healthier lifestyle in terms of diet, alcohol, exercise and consultations. regular medical care and smoking [...]. They can have goals and the confidence to achieve them that seem stronger. They also seem to be better able to solve problems and regulate their emotions in stressful situations "*.

Therefore, optimism has the power to guide an individual towards a healthy and balanced life with better management of emotions, which is beneficial for longevity. By being optimistic, we gain as much in quantity as in our quality of life.

We all know how much energy conflicts cost us: we are exhausted and weary after endless arguments and recurring wars. Psychological suffering is the bedrock of somatic illnesses, some of which could be very serious, greatly reducing life expectancy. And yet, many of us choose this path of self-destruction. We let emotions invade us and calm them with toxic products that slowly destroy us. We allow suffering to set in until depression and our willingness to seek happiness deteriorate.

Since we are travelling, let's ask ourselves the right questions: what's our flight plan? Where are we going? How to make this flight long and pleasant? How to choose quality partners to support us?

Nothing is ever too late. We are in our private jet and have full control over where and how to travel. The captain has just wished us a particularly good stay and is awaiting our instructions.

48
DO NOT SOW FEAR

Lately, the anxiety and fear around me seem to be increasing in intensity.

Catastrophic speeches multiply in conversations, on social networks and in my consultations. We are talking about the coronavirus epidemic that will decimate populations, and natural disasters as if they were never so terrifying.

On my Facebook page appear posts citing the Apocalypse announcing the end of the world, imaginary prophets who once again predict a bleak future for mankind.

Many people seem to take great pleasure in scaring others. When you say ten times a day that there are a few thousand more deaths, you can make millions of people tremble. It is more than profitable.

Technology and various means of communication make these things possible. We can fabricate fake news and escalate events to cause panic.

Some people may likely have a laudable goal, such as awakening human consciousness to leave darkness for light before it is too late. However, true spirituality is never acquired with fear of divine punishment, just an infantilizing belief.

Also, it is essential, in these times of doubt and an uncertain future, not to sow fear.

Fear only reinforces selfishness by activating the survival reflex to the detriment of the most fragile and destitute. It creates panic, discrimination, and shortages by obscuring common sense.

Only hope, peace, serenity, solidarity, love, and compassion deserve to be sown everywhere, in all hearts and always.

February 2020
Start of the coronavirus pandemic

49
REVEALING VIRUS

Back in the days when we ate "white bread," our world lived in a carefree way without asking too many existential questions. We knew some things were not going well, but as long as our health, our wallets, our family, and our friends were doing well, there was no need to worry anymore.

For the past few months, our world has been gradually shifting into its "black bread" period. A virus that has existed for millions of years in wild animals suddenly burst into our lives and exposed all our weaknesses.

It first showed us the fragility of human life and our equality in the face of disease. Rich or poor, powerful or weak, famous or unknown... There are no privileges for anyone in the pandemic.

It also revealed the errors of our materialist tendencies by wavering our models of society, our certainties of economic solidity, our political faults, our wasting of the available resources of the earth and our unconsciousness in front of its asphyxiation with the destruction of billions of its inhabitants.

However, although we always put daylight first, only the darkness of night can reveal what lies behind: the beauty of the moon and the twinkling of millions of stars.

So, the fear of dying reveals courage. The shortage underlines the nobility of sharing. The prospect of a bleak future tests the strength of our faith, optimism, and serenity.

The days of confinement strengthen the bonds between parents and children. They allow us to make up for lost time with our loved ones in our hectic life. They invite us to stay together and share what has been overlooked to date.

For some, they develop the richness of interior life through prayer, meditation, and a return to self.

Our planet has also taken the opportunity to take a deep breath, to detoxify a little from the pollution we impose on it. Many species of animals on land and at sea thrive, enjoying the sudden tranquillity afforded by confined humanity.

Hopefully, this pandemic marks the turning point of a world, selfish and cruel to one another, awakening us to the need to cooperate to keep the world clean and friendly.

Let it reveal the best part of each of us and the strengths that animate it: love, compassion, sharing, the courage to face adversity and make the necessary changes, as well as the wisdom to accept what we cannot change.

March 2020
Amid a coronavirus pandemic

50
BACK TO THE INNER SOURCE

According to the principles of oriental medicine, man is a small universe (microcosm) that must live according to the rules of the large universe (macrocosm).

After the big bang, the Universe splits into two parts. The visible part or the "form" (Yin) is represented by the celestial bodies (stars, planets…). It is distinguished from the invisible part or the "formless" (Yang), represented by the energy of the void occupying the rest of the universe.

With rotation around an axis being the general rule for celestial bodies, planets rotate, stars rotate, our sun revolves around itself, and the earth revolves around the sun, creating day, night and the four seasons that influence our lives and behaviours.

We work during the day and rest at night. Spring and summer, the bright Yang seasons which encourage activity, going out, joy… must be followed by autumn and winter, the dark Yin seasons which invite all nature to rest, to go inside, and invite us to meditation.

However, human activities tend to direct our lives towards an extreme Yang by the objectives of growth, productivity, sports performance, leisure, and pleasures constantly… to the detriment of Yin.

We no longer know how to stop, rest, and take care of our inner child, until the crash inevitably happens.

The Yin then sets in forcibly, forcing us to stop. This is the phenomenon of "burn-out", and "out of fuel". Everything was consumed following a Fire that lasted too long, energetically equivalent to a Yang taken to the extreme.

On a planetary scale, after an endless race for growth, a sign of a Yang exploited to the extreme, the coronavirus epidemic arrives as a Yin energy pushing humanity to slow down: global consumption is sharply reduced, pollution has started to drop dramatically around the world for the first time.

Let us take advantage of these Yin times of rest to get back to basics: the source of water that flows deep inside each of us, fresh and nourishing, which quenches thirst and relieves all burns.

51
THE PLUM TREE IN BLOOM

The plum tree in my garden, after rain, hail, and wind, whitens the courtyard with flower petals. It reminds me of a poem by Zen master Man Jue that I will try to translate below:

"When the spring goes away, hundreds of flowers fall.

On its return, it will hatch again.

The events of life pass before our eyes,
And signs of old age start appearing on the head.
Do not think all the flowers wither when spring goes away.
Yesterday evening, in the courtyard, a branch of a cherry tree was still blooming".

It is a poem about impermanence.
Things appear and disappear, come and go in perpetual cycles...
Never regret when something goes away. Another will come.
Let us live each moment intensely because it is unique and wonderful!

52
HE IS FREE, MAX

Since the coronavirus pandemic, many countries have adopted containment of their citizens to prevent the spread of the disease.

Some have been undergoing it for several weeks, others have just entered.

Suddenly, many of us realise the value of freedom: being able to travel, take family walks again, party with friends, or even just go out without that strange feeling of danger can come from anywhere, even from someone dear to our heart.

At a higher level, human beings need to be able to express themselves freely, give their opinion and demonstrate by respecting for others... without suffering any repression.

At an even higher level, vis-à-vis himself, he should be free to think without having a bad conscience to oppose an ideology, a dogma, a religious prohibition or to feel sinful, tainted by evil.

However, all of this does not yet represent the supreme freedom of the mind, that of renouncing an attachment.

Here is the story of Zen master Seung Sahn:

In the years 60-70, in the United States, youth tended to follow the Hippie movement, in which they wanted to live freely, without constraint, in more authentic human relationships. A hippie came to see Zen master Seung Sahn and said:

- I want to follow you for the lessons, but I want to keep my long hair which is the symbol of my freedom.

The master answered him:

- If you keep your hair long, it is because you are still attached to your freedom, so you are not free!

- All right, master, I am going to have my hair cut.

- Good! Now you can keep your hair long!

Indeed, an absolutely free mind can adapt to any situation, even to giving up its own freedom. It is like water that takes the form of its container, whether the latter is wide or narrow, harmonious, or misshapen.

If we reach this spirit, no door can be closed to us and no border can hold us back.

It reminds me of the words of a song by Hervé Christiani from the 80s: "He is free, Max. He is free, Max. Some even say they saw him fly… "

53
TAME LIFE

"He was standing before a garden, all a-bloom with roses.

"Good morning," said the roses.

The little prince gazed at them. They all looked like his flower.

"Who are you?" he demanded, thunderstruck.

"We are roses," the roses said.

And he was overcome with sadness. His flower had told him that she was the only one of her kind in all the universe. And here were five thousand of them, all alike, in one single garden! [...]

Then he went on with his reflections: "I thought that I was rich, with a flower that was unique in all the world; and all I had was a common rose. A common rose, and three volcanoes that come up to my knees--and one of them perhaps extinct forever... That doesn't make me a very great prince..."

And he lay down in the grass and cried.

It was then that the fox appeared.

"Who are you?" asked the little prince, and added, "You are very pretty to look at."

"I am a fox," the fox said.

"Come and play with me," proposed the little prince. "I am so unhappy."

"I cannot play with you," the fox said. "I am not tamed."

"Ah! Please excuse me," said the little prince.

But, after some thought, he added:

"What does that mean--'tame'?"

"It is an act too often neglected," said the fox. It means to establish ties".

"'To establish ties?'"

"Just that," said the fox. "To me, you are still nothing more than a little boy who is just like a hundred thousand other little boys. And I do not need you. And you, on your side, do not need me. To you, I am nothing more than a fox like a hundred thousand other foxes. But if you tame me, then we shall need each other. To me, you will be unique in all the world. To you, I shall be unique in all the world..." [...]

"And now here is my secret, a very simple secret: It

is only with the heart that one can see rightly; what is essential is invisible to the eye."

"What is essential is invisible to the eye," the little prince repeated so that he would be sure to remember.

"It is the time you have wasted for your rose that makes your rose so important."

"It is the time I have wasted for my rose--" said the little prince, so that he would be sure to remember.

"Men have forgotten this truth," said the fox. "But you must not forget it. You become responsible, forever, for what you have tamed. You are responsible for your rose . . .".

We often cry that we are not "a very great prince". We have so little compared to our neighbours who have happy families, to wealthy millionaires who are "full of money", to powerful politicians who have all the power, especially the power to steal what little we have. "The grass is always greener in the other fellow's yard"[6]. The situation is so unfair that it causes us to revolt with an anger proportional to our frustrations.

If only the fox from St Exupéry came back today to teach us how to "create links" with our world!

We would tame those around us with gentleness and patience and would give time to our sentimental, friendly, family, social and professional relationships.

We would create intimate bonds with our bodies to love them at their true value.

We would tame our living environment and would love it even in the face of adversity.

Thus, every little thing in our life would become

---
[6] by Raymond B. Egan and Richard A. Whiting, 1924

unique and would then take on invaluable value.

And then, the fox would recommend us to be "responsible" for what we have tamed, that is to say not to spoil relationships in the name of an oversized ego; not to destroy health to satisfy unfulfilled desires; not to betray the trust given to a given word; do not sacrifice respect, love, care for others in the name of any principle of equity or justice.

I am sure that if we followed in the footsteps of this wise fox, they would lead us to a new vision of our life, a vision more than extraordinary: we would see the invisible!

54
AWAKENING OF CONSCIOUSNESS

Being the living being at the highest level of consciousness, man often tends to take himself as the absolute master of the world by putting all nature at his service, treating other living beings such as animals and plants as objects without soul, without consciousness or intelligence.

However, it is enough to observe nature to understand that consciousness is omnipresent, its basic level, being the consciousness of existing, therefore of surviving. The first living things, the archaebacteria made up of a single cell, are already devising survival strategies in extreme conditions, followed by other extremophiles with amazing capacities to adapt to the most diverse and hostile environments. Today's bacteria are modifying their structures to resist the most modern antibiotics.

The world of plants is also astonishing. Plants transform themselves to avoid being destroyed by acquiring thorns, colours indicating toxicity. They attract bees and birds with smells, colours, nectar... to promote the dissemination of their pollen.

Recently, scientists discovered that forest trees communicate with each other through a dense underground network made up of roots and filaments of fungi. Thus, when a tree is attacked by a herbivore, it will change its chemical composition and diffuse this signal through this communication network, allowing its neighbours to guard against these attacks.

Many species, both vertebrates and invertebrates, know how to use camouflage to hide, or collective strength to protect themselves from danger. Birds already have the awareness of starting a family, choosing their mate, building their nests, protecting their eggs, and training the young to be independent. Evolved mammals have feelings, mourn the loss of the beings they love and can sacrifice themselves to save them.

Thus, all living things are conscious and connected to each other in a physical inter-existence and universal consciousness, each recycling what others have left, and this since the dawn of time. Indeed, nature did not know of waste before that produced by humans. Although all beings must live, they take from nature only what is necessary for them. They never intentionally destroy their living environment out of greed. They deserve our respect and our consideration and can even serve as a model for us to evolve.

Only by turning to oneself and without criticising others, do we awaken and reconnect to this universal consciousness of our original nature to find a harmonious life with all living beings.

55
THERE IS ONLY THE BEST

I remember a Chinese wisdom story that I read in my youth without understanding its meaning, until one day I awakened to Eastern spirituality:

A lady was going to the market to buy meat. She came to the butcher's stall and asked, "Could you give me the best bite you have?".

The latter replied: "On my stall, there is only the best!".

Imagine that this market stall is our life. Every day we would go there to seek what is best for us: love, soul mate, friends, children, health, social success, fame, money... all our dreams, in short. Some are happy with their visit, others very disappointed that they could not get what they wanted.

And yet, wisdom, represented by the image of the butcher, tells us: "On my stall, there is only the best!".

This story brings us to a new spirit, the

equanimous, non-discriminating spirit.

In Eastern spirituality, good and evil cannot be separated. It is the Yin-Yang duality, two sides of the same coin. In Yin, there is always Yang and vice versa. It is the image of two sides of the same mountain, one facing the sun, which is luminous (Yang), and the other remains in darkness (Yin).

As the earth revolves around the sun, the bright side will shift towards darkness and the dark side towards light. Nothing is permanent, everything changes, perpetually.

After the rain, comes fair weather. After the fair weather, comes the rain. Our life goes like this, immutably.

Let us not force the course of things. Let us be patient and prepare our minds to welcome what we want when it happens.

Let us not be disappointed if our goal is not achieved despite our best efforts. Let us not be sad if we are unable to hold onto what will fall apart. It could be a danger that we were able to avoid.

"What happens to us or doesn't happen to us is always the best. "Let us keep this conviction and we will walk through this life with a light heart as a breeze.

56
THE WORLD TAKES THE COLOUR OF YOUR EMOTIONS

Today a friend on Facebook, probably in a moment of sadness and disappointment posted these lyrics to a Renaud song, "Tired":

"Tired of living on planet Earth
On this bit of dust, on this shabby pebble
On this false star lost in the universe
Cradle of stupidity and realm of evil
Where the most evolved among creatures
Invented hate, racism, and war
And the cursed power that corrupts the purest
And get the wise man to spit on his brother".

Just to "counterbalance" a little this gloomy atmosphere that we meet very often at the moment, I offered him this poem whose verses are modelled on those of Renaud:

"Happy to live in the immensity of the Universe,
On this sea of sand, sparkling with stars,
On this rare diamond where life, although fleeting,
Very slowly, has woven its web;
Where the most evolved among creatures,
Aware of the damage caused by his emotions,
Seek to awaken the purest part,
Of his Spirit, universal, made of compassion.
Tirelessly, the voice of awakening, this sweet whisper,
Untie his ties and bring him out of his prison… "

I would like to offer it to you, hoping that your emotions will take on their colourful clothes every day!

57
AUTUMN ENERGY

We are in the fall. *"Dead leaves picked up by the shovelful, memories and regrets also"*. It is well known: when the sun has difficulty showing itself, hidden by the greyness and the incessant fine rain, the morale of humans is often at half-mast. Their energy is also at its lowest. This phenomenon is called "seasonal depression" or "winter blues". It affects 18% of Canadians, up to 9.7% of the adult population in North America and 4.6% of the European population.

The further one moves from the equator, the more the number of people affected increases.

In 1984, Dr Norman E. Rosenthal, psychiatrist and researcher at the National Institute of Mental Health, demonstrated the link between light and depression. This is because light rays act on neurotransmitters, including serotonin, the "happiness hormone" that regulates mood and governs the production of melatonin, another hormone responsible for wake-sleep cycles.

The lack of light, therefore, affects the secretion of these hormones and degrades our good mood.

If science discovered the influence of light on mood only in the middle of the 20th century, oriental medicine had understood it for thousands of years.

Indeed, it considers any living organism as a microcosm that should follow the same laws as the universe, the macrocosm. Light, heat, movement, joy, and going outside are Yang type energies. Darkness, cold, stillness, sadness, and staying in are Yin-type energies.

In summer, the sky is very bright, the temperature rises, so very Yang. Nature is on the move: insects abound, animals come out of their dens, vegetation is lush.

In autumn then in winter, the sky is grey, not very bright, the temperature drops, so very Yin. Nature gradually falls asleep: insects hide, animals hibernate, trees lose their foliage.

Therefore, the morale of the human being follows the Yin energy and "goes inside". He must rest like all living beings, to be able to "come out" stronger next spring.

Western medicine has found a cure for seasonal depression: light therapy. The patient is exposed to a wall of light for a few hours, and he gets better.

Energetically speaking, it is simply "bring more Yang" (ie, it is given the Yang it lacks), the light being Yang energy.

Others seek the sun abroad or go skiing (movement is also Yang energy). They will be better in winter but will be very tired next spring, having lost the necessary Yin time for rest.

Thus, we can consider that "seasonal depression" is energetically physiological. Let us learn to love the Yin, the rest inside, even with a little sadness during these rainy and cold months at the end of the year.

However, to balance the situation, we can always find comfort in a hot meal or herbal tea by the fireside, even in warm relations with family, with our friends... heat, being a Yang energy.

Living in harmony with the laws of nature is a habit of life that preserves longevity and serenity.

Article published in Carnets Comtois n° 42
Fall 2019

58
TWO SIMPLE CLUES

For oriental medicine, two main indices reflect the good mental health of an individual (and consequently his physical state of health since the two are intimately linked): to eat with appetite and to sleep with a restful sleep (without taking sleeping pills, of course) and without nightmare or dream.

It may seem simplistic at first glance, but in reality, obtaining these two clues requires a lot of conditions.

When we are overwhelmed with anxiety, consuming sugary foods temporarily helps calm the mind but can create a feeling of guilt for having put on weight that spoils the pleasure. In a devaluation of body image, food can be ingested in large quantities to fill an internally felt void, which can lead to eating disorders of the bulimic type. On the contrary, depression cuts your appetite by taking away all the pleasure of eating.

As for sleep, the question "do you sleep well at

night?", I am often answered with a "yes". On the other hand, if I insist on the quality of sleep by asking: "When you wake up in the morning, do you feel great, well recovered to start a new day? », The answer is often "no". Indeed, so many factors can affect the quality of sleep. Apart from somatic factors such as pain or sleep apnea syndrome, anxiety, nocturnal cogitation, excessive brain stimulation with television at night, video games, exciting substances (alcohol, coffee, etc.), fear of the next day, grief, depression... easily disturb sleep with difficulty falling asleep or frequent nocturnal awakenings.

If both of our indices are orange or even red, let us not take things lightly. This means that our mental balance is precarious and that we are under the pressure of our emotions without being able to control them.

It is a state of alert that should remind us of the need for regular training of the mind to let go and live in the present moment.

Day after day, month after month, we can use these two simple clues to gauge the progress of our mind on its journey towards balance and well-being.

59
THE ZEN SPIRIT IS NOT COMPLICATED

In ancient times, a practitioner asked a Zen master:
- Before your enlightenment, what were you doing?
The master replied:
- I cut wood, I carry water and I cook rice.
- And after your enlightenment, what did you do?
- I cut wood, I carry water and I cook rice.
- So what is the point of being enlightened?
- Before my enlightenment, when I cut wood, I think about carrying water. When I carry water, I remember to cook rice. After my enlightenment, when I cut wood, I think of cutting wood; when I carry water, I think of carrying water; when I cook rice, I think of cooking rice.

This mind is called mindfulness. To be there fully, right here and now.

It sounds simple, but many of us do not.

Our minds constantly wander between the past and the future and rarely stop at the present moment.

A few days ago, a patient told me: "Since the beginning of the year, I have been really worried about what will happen in the next few months!". I replied: "If you died tonight, you would have wasted eleven months of serenity of your life!".

Indeed, when a problem has a solution, why worry? When a problem does not have a solution, what is the point of worrying? Either way, let us let go of our emotions and deal with the problem to the best of our ability. The rest will come in due time or will not happen if it is not good for us.

It is with diligent and daily training of the mind that we can fully experience the present moment.

Hopefully one day we can all say, "When I think, I think; when I sleep, I sleep "and no longer" When I think, I sleep and when I sleep, I think ".

60
A WONDERFUL ILLUSION

Every day, the media reports cases of suicides of people who, no longer supporting their living conditions, prefer to put an end to them.

I have always considered the image of suicide to be that of a garbage truck in which waste accumulates over the years without ever having been emptied, just packed so that I can put a little more every day... until at the last garbage pick-up that tilts him into the void.

To every man, nothing is more precious than his own life. If we rule out the cases where the human is ready to sacrifice his own for another out of compassion or out of duty, the act of self-destruction is necessarily an error of judgement of the mind which considered that it was there. the only possible way to be delivered from his sufferings.

This mistake is the worst illusion of our life because it made us lose it.

Since childhood, we move from one illusion to another, with varying degrees of injury and scarring. We can cite a few:

"I was born to be happy", "I will be happy if I manage to do this job, to have a family, children, a lot of money, to be the one I want", "this is the love of my life. Without him/her my life is worth nothing!", "I should be healthy until my death", "my last departure will be predictable. Until then, I don't have time to think about it"... We can cite so many others, to the point of seeing that the very nature of our life is illusory.

When we go to the cinema, we know for a fact that what we are going to see is only an optical illusion resulting from millions of bright pixels putting together to form images, and that these images give the illusion of moving thanks to retinal persistence.

Knowing this, we are willing to pay for laughing, for being afraid, for being sad or angry, for all those emotions that make us come alive as long as they are fleeting and illusory.

What if, from now on, we look at our life as a wonderful illusion, a good movie, comedy or tragedy, in which we are spectators and actors?

We can then enjoy the joys and sorrows it gives us, lightly without ever sinking into the endless darkness of depression.

61
SALT STATUE

Genesis, the first book of the Old Testament, told the story of Sodom, a city of lust and debauchery. So, God decided to destroy this city, but he spared Lot, Abraham's nephew, who was a good man. The angels warned him and asked him to leave town with his family without looking back. Unfortunately, Lot's wife, unable to resist, turned and watched her past burn. She was instantly transformed into a pillar of salt.

Years of medical practice have brought me to numerous "salt statues" devastated by a past that prevents them from moving forward. Motionless "living-dead", unable to envisage a serene and happy future. Their thoughts, constantly turned to the past, gradually mummified, leading them to emotional anaesthesia, a heart incapable of feeling positive emotions, but only sadness and desolation.

Many have attempted a "return to the past" with psychoanalysis, hypnosis, and other mental techniques, seeking to understand the why and the how. Some get away with it, others get bogged down even deeper by constantly wiggling the knife in the wounds, sometimes with false memories and thus starting wars with their loved ones.

A Buddhist thought describes this situation well: "We are the work of our past and the architect of our future". Yes, our unhappiness today is indeed the consequence of our experience, sometimes by bad luck, but often by bad choices or ignorance. We have had wrong attitudes without realising their seriousness (word or deed) and create our own suffering by hurting others who defend themselves by retaliating, waging endless war and creating toxic relationships.

Maybe it is time to let go of the past, forgiving yourself and others, and then turning the page to build the future. The waste of yesteryear can be used as experiments, as compost to flourish the future in which we are architects today.

Let us be the salt that gives flavour to life, ours and that of those around us.

A few grains are enough. No need to make a whole statue of it.

62
THE LOOK OF THE OTHERS

To all those who suffer from the gaze and judgments of others, I would like to tell you a Zen story that could awaken us to a higher level of wisdom.

A king and a Zen master have been great friends for a long time. One day, to test the awakening of the Zen master, the king pretended to insult him to see if the latter would get angry:

- "You are not a Zen master, you are just a donkey!"

What was his surprise when the master answered him:

- "You are not just a king, you are a Buddha!"

We are often hurt by the looks, judgments, and comments of others when they are not in our favour. We feel demeaned, and insulted in our self-esteem, especially if we already lack self-confidence.

Some of us may suffer needlessly and spend years battling those around us with rage in our stomachs, torturing ourselves with this sense of injustice that repeats itself over and over.

However, by reacting violently to the opinions of others, we "validate" them as effective weapons (since they see that we are being affected) and allow evil people to use them to reach our egos.

What does this Zen story teach us?

1. An opinion coming from a person reflects who they are (their mentality, their education, their level of understanding, awakening...) and not who we are. We can respect it like any other opinion.

2. If we are hurt, it is just an impression of our ego. The bigger the ego, the more we will suffer. If the ego is transparent, all "bullets" will pass through it without any impact.

At a higher level, we will take advantage of the feedback of others to move forward.

With humility, let us examine them with discernment and improve our behaviour if the remarks are correct about us.

A donkey sees donkeys everywhere.
A Buddha sees Buddhas everywhere.
And us? What do we see everywhere?

63
THE «TCHING TCHONG» SALAD

One day, I unwittingly witnessed a small war on social media.

A famous chef, no doubt to bring humour to his guests, called his salad with Asian flavours "the Tching-Tchong salad".

This awkwardness, spotted on his menu by an Asian, had drawn the lightning of the whole community. Despite his apologies and the immediate withdrawal of the controversial name of his salad, hundreds of harsh criticisms continued to pour in on his page: accusations of racism, ignorance, calls to boycott his restaurant... Many even exceeded the subject concerned, accusing him of charging too high prices on his pastries, and so on.

Unable to let matters escalate, I stepped in to

defend him and calm things down.

Here is my plea for the restaurateur:

"I will try to take the time to explain my point of view to you. I have never denied anti-Asian racism in France. In my youth, I also had mockery and discrimination in the workplace.

However, with maturity, I understood that their authors often act in this way because they are also suffering and in fear of strangers, or out of total ignorance of our culture. Some have never travelled and only know clichés of Asians through Martial Arts movies or a few well-known dishes.

Words only have the value you give them. If you think "Tching Tchong" is an insult, it will be an insult and you will suffer. If you think these words are the phonetics of Respect[7], then they will not affect you.

I will conclude this story with an Asian joke: the idol of my youth, Bruce Lee, said in a film "wood does not kick" and I would not like to hear him add today "but salad do it!"

This intervention allowed me to see, through their arguments, that the most aggressive people in the lyrics are those who had suffered the most from racism in the past and that the wound is still gaping in them. This wound is like a seed buried in their unconsciousness. A joke, an awkwardness, an attitude, a word, or an act perceived as racist then arrives like a source of water that suddenly waters the seed. The plant of anger will grow, grow, reopen wounds, and amplify sleeping pain.

Awakening to the cause of suffering makes us understand that we are responsible for our own suffering and not for others. If we see a patch of

---

7   «Zun Zhong» 尊重 *in Chinese,* «Kính Trọng» *in Vietnamese*

mud on our cheek when we look in the mirror, it is pointless to clean the mirror to remove it. The mirror only reflects the stain that sits on our faces. It is by turning back to yourself that the good job of cleaning can begin. If we can dig up and remove the seeds of suffering from our minds once and for all, we will be untouchable.

Even as an Asian, I will be able to enjoy and laugh heartily at jokes about the way we speak, live, behave… without feeling targeted by their authors. Only my ego could be hurt. Without it, I will not have a problem anywhere.

This awakening can take us to an even higher level! Imagine that I know for a fact that my interlocutor is racist and is telling this joke on purpose to put me down and feel humiliated.

Without hindrance to my ego, my mind will develop compassion towards him: this man should not be happy! No happy person, who feels good about himself, would seek to hurt others. Maybe he was afraid of strangers or had suffered because of them and his pain is so bad that he should shower his antipathy on a stranger present near him, me in this case?

Either way, he needs help and if I can, I will help him.

You see, without ego, we will win everywhere: not only do we not suffer, but also we awaken to the suffering of others, to their frustrations and we develop our compassion necessary for our personal fulfilment.

So, let us let go of the name of this salad and fully appreciate its flavours!

Enjoy your meal!

64
WE ARE THE WICKED

I once asked the congregation in a seminar: "Who among you suffers because of the wickedness of others?". Almost everyone raised their hands.

Yet I am sure that if I now gather all those who have made my congregation suffer and ask them the same question, I will get the same rate of positive responses.

On reflection, we can realise that we always find ourselves on the side of the "good guys" who suffer from the wickedness of others. All wars in the world follow the same model: "the good against the bad". Of course, all fighters on both sides consider themselves to be part of the "axis of good" which fights evil.

This discriminating dual vision is the basis of

our suffering. We have always believed that light should overcome darkness without understanding where darkness comes from and how to overcome it. Suddenly, by fighting the darkness, we increase the dark part that is in us and that makes others suffer.

I will use an image to illustrate this: let's look at an empty yard in the sun. There is no shade, everything is bright. Let us now place ourselves in the middle of the courtyard: a shadow appears, ours. When the self appears, the light creates the shadow, regardless of the nature of the ego, good or bad.

Darkness and light are inseparable because they are not opposed. On the contrary, one allows the other to exist. Indeed, without night there will be no day and vice versa. This is the indiscriminate Yin-Yang duality of Eastern spirituality.

The spirit that delivers from suffering is the equanimous spirit, which does not judge, condemn, or hate. He understands that there are not purely "evil" people but only suffering or ignorant people. He knows that there are not purely "nice" people either, but only those who seek to awaken in compassion, their minds, still cluttered by the dust of the past, sometimes tilt them on the "dark side".

Today, let us try to ask ourselves this question: "What if we are the bad guys?". I am sure that everything can change in our life, fundamentally.

65
LITTLE LOVING ATTITUDES

I let a lady cross on the crosswalk. She waved to me to thank me and then accelerated the pace. She was almost running so as not to make me wait a few more seconds. She did not have to but did it naturally.

Driving in the car, a friend brakes lightly when she sees sparrows pecking on the road. She knows the risks of crushing them are minimal, but she does it automatically, as a gesture of natural protection for the animals she adores.

A young man bent down to pick up a twenty-euro bill that an elderly person had dropped from his pocket while taking out a handkerchief, without noticing it. He could have kept it, but he kindly returned it without hesitation.

A lady teaches her daughter not to choose all the

best-looking vegetables in a bin, to leave some for the next buyer. Not only does she not have to do this, but she also even taught her daughter it.

Open our eyes and we will see hundreds of small gestures as such in our daily lives.

They are much more rewarding for a man than his titles and diplomas than his fortune and his possessions. There is a big difference between being successful professionally and being successful in becoming a great man.

The real human value is seen through these loving little attitudes, executed naturally and silently because they do not serve to put the ego forward. They do not expect glorification, applause, or even any recognition.

However, although insignificant in the eyes of all, they are the real effective weapons to bring peace to the world, a world where humans cooperate with their neighbours and their environment to build their happiness and not kill each other for more. than its neighbour.

Jean-Henry Dunant (1828-1910), the founder of the International Red Cross said: *"Only those who are crazy enough to think that they can change the world succeed!"*

"It's a utopia," you might say.

And yet it just passed under my window this morning, in this sunny weather, in the hands of a little girl who was releasing the butterfly she had been trying to catch for a long time.

66
TONGLEN

Obviously, swimming with the current is much easier than going against the current.

In a time when men are suspicious of each other, where everyone is fighting for their own interests, the practice of "eye for eye, tooth for tooth" seems to be the norm.

When we are in pain, instead of solving our own problems, we tend to offload our discomfort on others and centre the notion of "good", and "just" on ourselves.

Surrender to revenge, to violence in word and deed is easy as if you are swimming in the same stream as everyone else. We are fighting our fight for survival in a world of wolves and sharks, what could be more natural?

However, if we follow this logic everyone will end up one-eyed and toothless. The pain and resentment will persist over and over again.

Today I would like to tell you about a practice equivalent to swimming against the tide, which originated in Tibetan Buddhism, Tonglen.

Etymologically, "Tonglen" means "to give and to receive".

It is quite easy to practise by meditating (while washing the dishes, standing in front of a red light, stuck in a traffic jam, in a queue at the supermarket, or quietly in an armchair at home...):

- By inhaling very slowly, think: *"I inhale with compassion all my suffering (towards my inner child) / all your suffering (towards a specific person) / all the suffering in the world (vis-à-vis humanity) to transform it".*

- Exhaling very slowly, think: "I *am exhaling peace and benevolence so that compassion can transform me / you / transform this world".*

With the regular practice of Tonglen, our mind, which is usually a landfill where garbage has accumulated for years, will turn into a recycling plant where every waste will be transformed into a work of art, for our happiness and other people's.

Tonglen will help us to heal our inner child, to gradually dissolve our ego.

It will teach us to adopt an increasingly optimistic view of the world around us.

Believe it or not, over time you can even tame sharks and dance with wolves.

Every time you meet someone in your life, you

will leave an imprint in their heart by awakening the kindness that lies within them.

And the world will be at peace, just like in one of your dreams!

67
THE SONG OF THE ROOSTER

We have all heard a rooster crowing, no matter where we live.

While it is obvious that the rooster crows the same way in every corner of the globe, its song is heard by no means the same by all people.

Thus, the Vietnamese rooster uses a single vowel but with tones: "ò ó o ooo". The French rooster adds consonants to make a "cocorico". The American rooster is a linguist: "cock-a-doddle-do". His Irish counterpart is a qualified speech therapist, able to sing: "mac na hóighe slán".

As a child, I read in a book that a rooster from an African country would sing "tongazoki oo". In short, if you do some research on the Internet, you will see as many rooster crows as there are existing countries.

This little story makes you smile but contains a profound lesson.

Each time we hear a noise, a song, a word, a story..., its content passes through a filter before arriving at its final interpretation by our brain.

This filter is the result of our culture, our customs, our education, our own life experiences, and our emotional state of the moment... It is called "ego vision" because it is systematically used by our ego to forge itself. an opinion on others, on society, on the world, on good and evil, moral and immoral, justice and injustice... He judges, condemns and discriminates.

It is the starting point for misunderstandings, discords, conflicts, and wars.

What we think is right and logical is not necessarily for our interlocutor, each having their own egotistical vision. Our references are not his and vice versa.

So, when a word or story hurts us deeply, let us look at it with a clear mind to recognize the responsibility of the egotistical seeing in our suffering.

The further we move away from it, the less we will suffer.

With this awakening, we will never hear a rooster crow the same way again, for it is... just like this!

68
PLEASE CALL ME BY MY TRUE NAMES

I would like to share with you this magnificent poem by Vietnamese Zen master Thich Nhat Hanh.

Several decades ago, when I took my first steps on the path to Zen, reading it had shaken me greatly, to the point of crying bitter tears.

He opened my eyes to the inter-existence of all beings in the "Great Whole", the original Emptiness, whatever their forms, their means of existence, their ways of life, their degree of ignorance, which creates suffering in others.

He strongly pushed the doors of compassion into my heart and pointed me to the path of the bodhisattvas, those who have vowed to help other sentient beings awaken as long as there are any left in this world.

Even today, every time I read this poem in front of a congregation, in Buddhist retreats, the emotion still squeezes my throat, and a tear always flows discreetly from my eyes.

This poem was put into song and sung in the Plum Village; a Buddhist community founded by master Thich Nhat Hanh.

I invite you to read it and reread it, until you feel all its deeper meaning and its wonderful beauty.

*«Don't say that I will depart tomorrow -
even today I am still arriving.*

*Look deeply: every second I am arriving
to be a bud on a Spring branch,
to be a tiny bird, with still-fragile wings,
learning to sing in my new nest,
to be a caterpillar in the heart of a flower,
to be a jewel hiding itself in a stone.*

*I still arrive, in order to laugh and to cry,
to fear and to hope.
The rhythm of my heart is the birth and death
of all that is alive.*

*I am a mayfly metamorphosing
on the surface of the river.
And I am the bird
that swoops down to swallow the mayfly.*

*I am a frog swimming happily
in the clear water of a pond.
And I am the grass-snake
that silently feeds itself on the frog.*

I am the child in Uganda, all skin and bones,
my legs as thin as bamboo sticks.
And I am the arms merchant,
selling deadly weapons to Uganda.

I am the twelve-year-old girl,
refugee on a small boat,
who throws herself into the ocean
after being raped by a sea pirate.

And I am also the pirate,
my heart not yet capable
of seeing and loving.

I am a member of the politburo,
with plenty of power in my hands.
And I am the man who has to pay
his "debt of blood" to my people
dying slowly in a forced-labor camp.

My joy is like Spring, so warm
it makes flowers bloom all over the Earth.
My pain is like a river of tears,
so vast it fills the four oceans.

Please call me by my true names,
so I can hear all my cries and laughter at once,
so I can see that my joy and pain are one.

Please call me by my true names,
so I can wake up
and the door of my heart
could be left open,
the door of compassion.»

         Zen master Thich Nhat Hanh

69
SEE THE INVISIBLE

The 21st century is the century of medical imaging. Technological advances in this field give unparalleled power hitherto to modern medicine. The human body can be cut into thin slices and reconstructed in all planes in 3D. The visible lesions are thinner and thinner. Functional MRI makes it possible to visualise brain activity in real- time, recording local variations in the properties of cerebral blood flow when these areas are stimulated.

We can think that soon, the algorithms will be able, from the activated areas of our brain, to guess our mental state (calm or stressed), our thoughts, and why not, our intentions.

Maybe one day we will even invent the "Lovemetre" applied to the chest to measure the intensity of our love for someone, whose unit will be the "Lov".

I see the headlines of the newspapers of the future:

"Thanks to the 7G, he sent 2000 Lov to his lover living at 13,000 km in 1 / 10th of a second", or even " A patient urgently admitted to the hospital: a shock of 10,000 anti-Lov broke her heart", or even " Hurt by her jealous spouse because her lovemetre shows a negative score "... It is terrifying, isn't it?

Rest assured, this is just a sci-fi movie born out of my neural delusions tonight! There are things that we will never be able to measure because they belong to the realm of the subtle, such as love, human relationships, emotions, and suffering...

Yet, every day, many patients want to perform scans or MRIs to "see" what is wrong with their brain or their body, to explain the symptoms of the deep discomfort that they have been dragging for years without a valid solution, the drugs being all ineffective.

Saint-Exupéry had rightly said: *"It is only with the heart that one can see rightly; what is essential is invisible to the eye".*

However, to see with the heart, we need its intelligence, which is based on empathy, compassion, and emotional understanding.

The intelligence of the heart is the only one that will know how to distinguish suffering from wickedness, love from attachment, letting go of indifference, acceptance to submit, and true deliverance from the change of master to serve.

It arises from spiritual awakening, is subtle and not measurable by an Intelligence Quotient.

It is this alone that makes the greatness of being, beyond all visible appearance.

70
THE EMPTY MIND (HEART)

If you go to Obaku temple in Kyoto, you will see the words *"The First Principle"* engraved above the door. The letters of this inscription are unusual in size, and calligraphy enthusiasts consider it a masterpiece of its kind. It was designed by Zen master Kosen two centuries ago.

Here is his story:

"Master Kosen applied himself to making his calligraphy on a large paper which will be given to the engraver to reproduce it on the wood. As he did so, stood beside him a cheeky pupil, who had prepared several litres of ink for this purpose and did not hesitate to criticise his master's work.

- This calligraphy is not beautiful, he said after the first sketch.

- And this one?
- No more. It is even less beautiful than the first.

Kosen patiently blackens eighty-four sheets, none satisfying his student.

Finally, as the young man had been away for a few moments, Kosen said to himself: "Here is my chance to escape his critical eye" - and he hastily traced "The First Principle", without being distracted by the presence of the student. When the latter returned, he exclaimed:
- This is a masterpiece, Master!

Let us take advantage of this story to understand one of the fundamental notions of Zen: "The Empty Mind (Heart)". When we perform an action (outside of the automatic tasks performed as part of our work), we usually aim for two things:

1. Calm an emotion that grips our mind: anger, fear, anxiety, sadness, frustration, shame, regret...

2. Satisfy our ego by showing others our strength, our abilities, our talents, our courage, our kindness, our beautiful image... to collect congratulations, admiration or thanks, often unconsciously.

As a result, the action often misses its real purpose. Many of us can even miss a good chunk of our lives by always wanting to please others, conform to standards, or on the contrary fight anything and everything, anyone to assuage a deep emotional discomfort.

If our only engine is compassion for the other, without the ego's demand for a "return on investment", our Heart / Mind becomes empty, and the action will be spontaneous and aimless.

At that point, everything can be created in a perfect way.

71
THE BLACK NOSE BUDDHA

Among the Zen stories that have been passed down for centuries is one of a nun who spent her life seeking supreme grace from the Buddha. She asked a craftsman to make her a small statue of Buddha covered with gold leaf which she took everywhere on her pilgrimage routes.

One day, she arrived at a small temple in a village with multiple statues of Buddha enthroned on the altar.

To prevent the smell of her incense sticks from reaching the other Buddhas, she made a small funnel to direct the smoke directly to hers. After a while, his Buddha's nose turned black as coal.

When living conditions become difficult, the survival reflex aggravates selfish tendencies. The "me", then the "mine", the "ours" become clearer and clearer when shortages arrive, to the detriment of all common sense.

No matter how much we talk about sharing and altruism, the fear of missing out brings us closer to the reptilian "fight or flight" behaviour that has been in our genes since the dawn of time.

Out of ignorance, we worsen our condition and condemn the most vulnerable.

Let us take a step back and look deep inside. The most difficult times in our lives are tests that measure the importance of our ego, directly proportional to our suffering.

When the blind "me" is there, nothing else takes precedence. Advice, and even the sincerest prayers, are funnelled into our own needs, our own survival.

The nose of our inner golden Buddha then becomes quite visible, blackened by the hard-to-erase soot of the ego.

72
A TRUE DONATION, A TRUE HELP

One day, while walking through a market on his way back to the monastery, a young monk noticed that a vendor had captured many frogs and put them in a cage to display them to passers-by. Listening only to his heart, the young monk emptied his pockets, bought all the frogs and let them go to a stream. Running back to the temple, he proudly told his master, "Master, I have freed all the frogs." However, the latter, contrary to his expectations, did not give him congratulations. Noticing his astonished look, the master then explained to him: "It's because you said it was you who freed them".

One of the most common sufferings is when a person feels unfairly treated by others despite all the help they have given them over the years. I hear this outrageous speech very often: "When they needed me, I was always there. I never say "no" when asked for help. *Too good, too stupid*". *Now that I need the others, there is no one to help me. Enough, I do not want to be there for anyone, anymore! I do not understand why this is not right. But what's wrong?*"

I am going to use the words of the Zen master to explain to you: "It is because you said that it was you who helped them!"

The "me" is that extra word that plunges us into suffering. When the ego is there, our giving is not free, our help is not selfless or unconditional. Subconsciously, we become creditors, we lend with the expectation that we can get our update back one day, and sometimes at a small profit. We delude ourselves with our image of benevolent, saviour, a pillar on which everyone can lean… and we suffer disappointment and become embittered when the reaction of those around us is not what we expect.

The truth is, a donation can only be completely free if it does not put the donor in need. Our help can only be completely selfless if we are fully sufficient in ourselves.

"The frogs are freed", and "those who suffer are helped".

Who is behind all of this? Nobody.

Just love, or compassion, should be shared when it is full and overflowing.

This is our true nature, and it is not closed by the boundaries of the self.

73
THE FIFTH DIMENSION

"It's a beautiful novel, it's a beautiful story... He was going home, up there towards the fog, she was going down to the South. They found themselves on the side of the road, on the vacation highway. It was probably a lucky day. They had the sky at their fingertips. A gift from providence... "

We all know this beautiful song by Michel Fugain where love is born from a chance meeting between a man and a woman whose paths crossed at some point in their lives.

If we examine the conditions necessary for this instant to exist, we will see that the usual three dimensions of space are not enough. Indeed, their roads could very well cross geographically, but a few minutes of delay is enough for they never met. This fourth dimension is that of time and more precisely of "synchronism": the two protagonists must be in the same place at the same time. However, they still lack a fifth dimension that we call "synchronicity": if one of them is not on hold, is not free, or is not ready to start a relationship, their love will not be able to be born even if they are face to face.

Synchronicity highlights invisible bonds that bind everything together in Oneness, but which are dissolved when we close the boundaries of the self, creating Duality between "me" and "the others". Understanding this notion of synchronicity is fundamental to lightening our life. Indeed, we are always waiting for a lot of things, impatient to see them happen and disappointed not to see them happen or materialise.

Being in synchronicity with the universe means having the patience to wait for the right moment when your dreams will come true, just as avoiding eating fruits when they are still green. To be in synchronicity with the universe is also to accept that certain desires cannot be satisfied for lack of this fifth dimension, and to continue to hold the conviction that whatever happens or does not happen is always the best.

But being in synchronicity with the universe is all about preparing to be ready when the opportunity presents itself.

So, every day we ask ourselves this question: "Am I ready to embrace my dream when it arrives?" And we will see that we will always be missing one last shoe to slip on at the long-awaited time.

74
BREATHE AND COME BACK AT HOME

When the future seems dark to you
In a sad and anxious world,
Losing its blue colour,
Locking you in his worst torments.

Breathe and come home,
In your beautiful and solid home
Where it is mild in the four seasons,
Where joy and happiness are kept.

When the emotional waves follow one another,
Wounding you with their incessant strikes,
On the horizon, you see no help,
Only loneliness is still present.

Breathe and come home.
Gently close the door and leave
Storms and threats, all these illusions,
Outside and far from your fortress.

When the past traps your thoughts,
Preventing you from taking the slightest step.
His demons bury your freedom
and keep your sufferings in their arms,

Breathe and come home,
Where a wonderful love awaits you,
Where mindfulness, compassion, and wisdom,
Will help you build a happy future too.

75
REALLY?

Zen master Hakuin lived in a city in Japan. He was highly regarded, and many people came to listen to him impart his spiritual teachings. One day, her neighbour's teenage daughter got pregnant. Her parents of the latter got angry and berated her for knowing the identity of the father. The girl finally confessed to them that it was Hakuin. The angry parents rushed to his house screaming that their daughter had confessed that he was the child's father. He answered them: "Really?"

Word of the scandal spread throughout the city and beyond. The master lost his reputation, and no one came to see him anymore. But that did not seem to shake Hakuin who remained impassive as if this story did not concern him.

When the child was born, the parents took him to Hakuin saying, "You are the father, so take care of it!". The master took great care of the child and went everywhere to beg for milk for him.

A year later, taken with remorse, the young girl confessed to her parents that the real father of the child was a young man who worked at the butcher. Alarmed and distressed, the parents went to Hakuin's to ask his forgiveness: "We are so sorry. We came to pick up the child. Our daughter confessed that you were not the father ". The master answered them by handing them the baby: "Really?".

Sometimes we feel like life is going after us. We simply wish to lead a quiet life, without history and here is that the troubles come incessantly not giving us a single moment of respite: accidents, illnesses, unemployment, family conflicts, professional, slander, slander, judgments, mockery...

Our world seems to be turning in the wrong direction, the one we reject with all our might.

And we struggle, again and again... to restore truth and justice, to cry out our rage for being unlucky, here and now.

Some of us, nostalgic, regret a past magnified by the imaginary. Others, pessimists, are already afraid of a bleak and hopeless future.

We want to show that we are strong and solid like the Oak in La Fontaine's fable, always standing through thick and thin, until the day we admit defeat, uprooted and bitter forever, crushed by this ruthless outside world.

Eastern spirituality adopts the opposite attitude,

that of the Roseau which bends in the storm, accepting lies and truths, luck and bad luck, justice or injustice as two facets of the same illusion. This is neither cowardice nor indifference or even resignation or fatalism.

Master Hakuin simply saw that at that point in his life he had to meet this child, raise him, and love him. Without it, maybe the first year of his life, rejected by his mother and grandparents, would have been much less rosy. This is how it should be. They still make sense, even if we do not see them yet.

Everything else (reputation, self-esteem, feelings of injustice...) are just needs of the ego, and therefore irrelevant to it.

If we can keep a balanced mind in the face of every event in our life and accept the two sides of light and dark that coexist, we will ride through all these obstacles and storms with serenity.

" Really?"

The truth is just like this.

76
RISING

Mr P. came for a consultation a few days ago, in a sorry state. Embittered and disappointed after many lost fights to restore justice, he plagues everything around him: the world, society, government, people, his family, his children... Nothing seems to find favour in his eyes. His voice carries the tone of anger, denouncing the deceit of the human being, the social injustices, the frustrations at the stupidity and ingratitude of those close to him. His language includes only violent words, calling others bird names and revealing deep frustrations.

After a long discussion, he finally admitted that he had cleared his surroundings by having a "heavy hand" when he felt criticism and animosities towards him. He tried in vain to make efforts to improve his relations. His life is like a labyrinth where he goes around in circles, surrounded by problems.

I told him about a method of working the mind that might help him get out of this: rising!

Raising in vision consists in looking not only at the "bad" side of events and beings but also at their luminous side to acquire a more global point of view of reality.

Raising in thought is about viewing events and beings "as they are", without prejudice or value judgement to help the mind strive for equanimity.

Raising in speaking is about removing all harsh, hurtful, violent, deceptive, and manipulative words from one's vocabulary and using their power to comfort, encourage and bring peace, reconciliation, and love.

Raising in action is to fight peacefully against injustice around you with compassion as your only weapon, without anger or hatred in your heart, cultivating patience and tolerance. This way, lost hearts will never leave you bitter again. They will not diminish the courage to return to the front, starting by fighting the main adversary in us, our ego.

As we rise above the labyrinth of our lives, we will easily see dead ends to avoid and the best paths to take.

In addition, a peaceful and light heart, freed of its leaden cover, will be our reward!

77
LES VENTS DE LA VIE

Su Dong Po, a great poet of the Song Dynasty, is a great friend of Zen master Fo Yin. A diligent practitioner, he often sought to prove to Fo Yin that he had reached a high level of mastery of his mind.

One day, he sent a beautiful poem to the Zen master describing the state of an enlightened mind, which remains motionless despite the squalls of the "8 Winds".

In Buddhist teaching, the "8 Winds" which can make the mind waver are:

. Greed for material goods,
. Excessive regret for losses,
. Hurt by others' judgements,
. Satisfaction with the praise of others,
. Proud of the honours received,
. Anger of slander towards oneself,

. Rejection of uncomfortable situations
. Search for pleasant stimuli.

Knowing his friend and to test his mind, Fo Yin sends the poem back to him with a comment: "Just a fart!".

Receiving the letter, Su Dong Po got angry and crossed the river by himself to go to the monastery.

Seeing it, he yelled, "What did you find wrong in my poem to judge it like this?"

Fo Yin replied mischievously: "In your poem, you talk about the spirit that does not move despite the squalls of the '8 Winds'. And there, only one "little wind" has already made you cross the river!".

Su Dong Po burst out laughing, understanding the teacher's lesson.

In recent times, I have witnessed a lot of suffering in my consultations. There were those encountered at work, where many people bring their personal discomfort there to unload it on their colleagues or their subordinates. There were also those from family conflicts, interminable disputes that end in violence, complaints, lawsuits and wars between separated parents where children are hostages and victims.

We are constantly suffering from the squalls of these "8 Winds", which at first glance all seem to come from others, from our toxic environment.

However, if we have the courage to look at our suffering with clarity, we will see that these emotional storms all arise from our untrained mind, which attaches itself to ego wounds and cannot free itself from them.

Real change does not come from outside, but in soothing our own minds through letting go.

Do not cross the river for a little wind.

We just have to smile, now that we know the trap!

78
ALIMENTARY, MY DEAR WATSON !

Summer is the season when food takes pride of place in our society. Holidays, parties, family meals, with friends... lead us to overeat. Conversely, swimsuits and scales make us lean towards moderation. The television and magazines praise local specialities, organic products, recipes from chefs... who invite us to eat healthy and balanced while keeping the pleasure.

I would like to take this opportunity to tell you about two other "food" levels that some people forget, but which are also essential for our balance.

The first is "intellectual foods". Our brains tend to take the easy way out. A video game, with its breathtakingly beautiful images and rich storylines, a good action or sentimental film often seems to be enough to feed our brains, which are always thirsty for new things.

However, with hindsight, we can see that this world is well limited by the programming of its designers and does not allow us to dream beyond their creativity.

Albert Einstein had given his opinion on children's brains: "if you want to have intelligent children, read them fairy tales! And if you want them to be really smart, read them fairy tales!"

Why? would you tell me. Because our imagination goes far beyond the story, the setting and the characters created by the author. Indeed, we are often disappointed when our childhood story turns into a movie, the latter always being less beautiful than we imagined.

Books make us dream and travel. They open our vision to the world, to customs, to people we have never met. They feed our imagination and our creativity and bring us closer to different currents of thought and points of view. We acquire the intelligence of the heart by understanding the inner workings of this world. Culture (including art) is thus an excellent food for our brain.

On an even higher level, our happiness will be perfect with spiritual nourishment. It is food that brings us towards self-realisation by gradually freeing us from our excess emotions, our loss of control in front of others, our excess of language and our spontaneous actions which create suffering in those around us.

These products are even more "terroir", since they are found within us, carried by our inner child whom we often tend to abandon to run behind trivialities.

Finally, to maintain a balance at all levels, it is just alimentary, my dear Watson!

79
TWO SPECIAL DAYS

The Dalai Lama once gave this wonderful teaching: "There are two days in a life when nothing can be done: yesterday and tomorrow."

Rather than advising us to "live the present moment" or "to be here and now", he shows us that this is not a recommendation, but an observation: we cannot help but live the moment. present, here and now.

The idea is simple: the past is already over. He is behind us. There is nothing more we can do to change or improve it.

As for the future, what we plan to do in the near future is pure speculation for now! Who among us can say that he/she will still be alive on that date, or how things will turn out?

Today is the only day when we can right the mistakes of the past and prepare for the future, accepting that the results will not necessarily be what we want.

Today is also the day when we reap what we have sown in the past. Those who had planted wheat can now eat bread. Those who had grown potatoes can enjoy their fries. Those who had neglected the care of their gardens find themselves with nothing.

Here there is no comparison or value judgement. Every tree has its fruits. The choices we made in the past are reflected in the present and we must take responsibility for them.

However, our minds are often far from understanding this evidence. He wanders endlessly in the past with regrets. He sets up "if" scenarios: If only this, that had been different, or it could have been better.

At the same time, he travels to a distant future, uncertain and a source of anguish.

Thus, most of us forget to live the present fully and also forget to prepare for the future with serenity.

"They live as if they were never going to die... and die as if they had never lived" noted the Dalai Lama.

So, at this point, let us come back to our inner child through conscious breathing. Let us be awake to the fact that we are the work of our past and the architect of our future.

Let our minds rest from these two special days and work with joy and fullness in building this present moment.

This is how our future will be wonderful and transcendent.

80
A HANDFUL OF SALT

One day, a woman came before Shakyamuni Buddha and asked him:

"Master, someone wronged me twenty years ago, but I still can't forgive him. Every time I think about this fact, anger always rises in me. I cannot let go. What should I do?"

The Buddha replied, "If you throw a handful of salt into a glass of water, the water becomes undrinkable. However, if you throw the same handful of salt into a river, as it is vast and constantly flowing, the water will still be drinkable".

Often when we are angry, our minds fill with the image of the alleged culprit and his trespasses against us. Our ego automatically searches for words of retaliation, even avenues of attack and revenge.

Our double, ignorant and heartless Mr Hyde comes back in force and replaces the kind Dr Jekyll in our thoughts.

Our mind fixes the story, clings to it, and makes everything still and immutable, like that glass of water into which we have just thrown a handful of salt. The purity of the water is wasted. It will be permanently salty and undrinkable. This injustice is unbearable, and reparation is called for.

In this little tale, the Buddha reminds us of two facts:

First, the raison d'être and the duration of our anger depend on our greatness of soul. If the compassion that dwells in our hearts is as large as a river, an offence cannot change its nature. The anger will dissolve quickly, and the water will remain drinkable and thirst-quenching. We will be able to forgive, to let the emotions go away quickly, without being strongly affected by them.

Some of us find it difficult to have toxic relationships with those around us. To forgive does not mean to accept these conditions of life. We can choose to separate ourselves from people who ignore their own suffering and unload their frustrations on others at the slightest opportunity. However, we can keep our hearts away from any hatred or desire for revenge that we will be the first to suffer.

Each tree has its fruits. We only must take care of our own garden.

The Buddha also reminds us of an often-forgotten truth: the impermanence of everything! Unlike water in a glass, that of the river of our life flows to the ocean without ever turning back. The past, even awfully close, is over. Bringing with you all your bad memories, torments, resentments... only spoils the present moment and the future to come.

Knowing how to turn the page, move towards renewal and recreate peace and harmony always will allow us to always remain serene in the inevitable storms of the human condition.

May the handfuls of salt be trials that make us humbler, more understanding, more human.

That they make our hearts larger, our egos smaller, and our happiness more selfless.

81
EVENING MEDITATION

I sit.
Just twenty minutes.
A long day has just ended,
With so many drawers not yet closed,
But I am already tired:
- Business to settle tomorrow, the day after tomorrow, later...
- Emotions dragged on for hours: anger, stress, regrets, weariness...
- Frustrations, "why" and "if"
- The fears of the next day: work, colleagues, bosses...

I breathe in slowly, deeply and my abdomen swells... coming back to yourself, to the present moment.

I breathe out slowly, deeply and my abdomen retracts... I return peace and kindness to myself.

I close the drawers, one by one:
- Each day suffices for its sorrows. I leave tomorrow's work for tomorrow.
- I calm my emotions. They are illusory and ephemeral. I create them, I turn them off. I am the only master on board.
- I accept my frustrations. No "why" or "if". Life always has the best in store for me.
- Tomorrow, I will be better able to manage my relationships with a smaller ego. I will apologise and fix my mistakes.

I breathe in slowly, deeply and my abdomen swells...
I am happy to be here and now. Let go.

I breathe out slowly, deeply and my abdomen retracts... I wish to awaken to all those I love and those that I still have difficulty understanding and accepting.

My drawers are closed. I gradually relax all my muscles, from head to toe.
I am ready to go to bed.

I breathe in slowly, deeply and my abdomen swells...
I feel deep gratitude after this busy day.
I breathe out slowly, deeply and my abdomen retracts... I send peace to all living beings.

Good night, Universe, I join you.

82
HOSTILITY

I have known her for a long time. Whenever she comes in for consultation, it is in "warrior mode" against anyone besides her.

She is always tense, even enraged and never satisfied.

For her, the world represents a permanent threat to her person, which justifies her hostile attitude towards those around her: her partner first (who has just run away), then her boss and her co-workers arrive.

As soon as she arrived, she began to talk about their misdeeds, often in an accusing tone, sometimes mockingly, followed by threats of reprisals from her. Her hostility towards those around her is such that even their benevolent gestures are interpreted as manipulation. I can only remain silent and listen to her, so as not to be accused in my turn of complacency vis-à-vis her enemies.

I know she is in pain from her ego wounds. As long as she does not realise that her problems stem from her behaviour, the road to deliverance may still be long, exceptionally long...

According to a study published in the journal EJCN (European Journal of Cardiovascular Nursing), hostility could be considered a risk factor for the recurrence of heart attacks. To reach this conclusion, doctors at the University of Tennessee in Knoxville followed 2,321 patients with previous myocardial infarction for 24 months.

Their hostility was first measured using a questionnaire called MAACL (Multiple Adjective Affect Checklist), which measures personality traits. The average age of the participants was 67 years old. 68% of men and 57% of women were classified as hostile by the personality test.

"Hostility is a personality trait that includes being sarcastic, cynical, resentful, impatient or irritable", says Dr Tracey Vitori. "It's not just a one-off occurrence but characterises how a person interacts with people".

In her view, improving the character and behaviour of myocardial infarction patients, such as quitting smoking or playing sports, is a way to take control of their lifestyle and thus avoid the risk of recurrence.

Again, the ego is largely responsible for our emotional disorders. It affects our body and drastically reduces our length and quality of life.

The ego is not us, because it does not love us!

Let us reduce it and regain confidence in ourselves, then in others.

The world is not a battleground, and our bodies are not necessarily a victim of war, unless we allow it!

83
SOUL WINDOWS

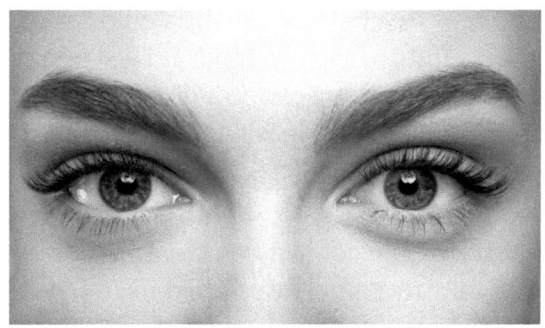

In 1989, researchers Kellerman, Lewis, and Laird published an interesting article in the Journal of Research in Personality, titled *"Watching and Loving: The Effects of Mutual Gaze on Feelings of Romantic Love"*.

Forty-eight pairs of students gathered to look each other eye-to-eye for two minutes after chatting for a little while. At the end of the experience, many of them fell in love. There were even two marriages celebrated six months later. Most participants admitted to feeling more attracted to each other, despite not knowing each other half an hour earlier!

Indeed, from our childhood, eye contact is already an essential means of communication. The more parents express their love by looking at their child's eyes, the more the child will be able to nourish himself emotionally and develop harmoniously. Many of us have the habit of looking the child in the eye just to argue with him or to congratulate him.

By doing this, we are unconsciously giving the child a sign of conditional love (= he should be in such and such a condition to catch the eyes of the parents) and might cause him to feel that he is not unconditionally loved. Worse, some parents use the refusal to look the child in the eye as a form of punishment. Psychologically, this could be devastating for his future because the child will adopt this behaviour later towards those around him, his spouse and then his children. He will thus create other misunderstandings, conflicts and even rejection around him.

Indeed, the lack of eye contact can create visible disabilities. A usually misunderstood child becomes anxious and fearful. He does not dare to look straight in the eye and only glances stealthily to observe the reactions of others. He will eventually pull away from others and lock himself into his relationship and learning difficulties for a lack of self-confidence.

It is often said that the eyes are the windows to the soul. That is true. A great love story happens when a boy asks a girl, "Do you love me? » And she answers him: « Look in my eyes ». A deep, loving gaze is worth more than a thousand words.

The researchers found that 3.2 seconds is the amount of time participants could look a stranger in the eye without feeling uncomfortable. Thus, accepting to sustain a gaze over time means opening the windows of one's soul to the other and at the same time observing one's inner world. It is also showing your vulnerability by accepting trust. For this reason, eye contact may be the start of a great story... or not.

However, before opening our windows, let us make sure that our interior house is beautiful, free from the waste of resentment, discrimination and hatred. Let us decorate it with love and generosity.

In these times of virtual contact, mainly via smartphones, the internet, and masked smiles, we offer our compassionate and warm gaze to others.

It is an exceptional gift that could change the world.

84
LET GO

Two monks walked along a river toward their monastery. They did a mindful meditative walk, focused on each step.

Suddenly, they saw a young girl completely distraught. She wanted to ford the river but was afraid of being swept away by the strong current.

Without hesitation, the oldest of the monks placed the young girl on his back, crossed the river and deposited her on the other bank. He then rejoined his companion, and both resumed their journey in silence.

An hour later, unable to restrain himself any longer, the younger monk questioned his elder with a gloomy expression: "Venerable, you have broken a precept, we have no right to touch a woman and even less to carry her on our back".

The old monk looked at his young friend with a compassionate smile and retorted, "My young friend, I have dropped the young girl at the other river bank for an hour. Why are you still carrying it in your mind?"

In our life, we are no different from this young monk. For years, we have been dragging around in our minds various cumbersome things that spoil our serenity at every moment: unresolved disputes, resentments, the anger of injustice, ego wounds, dissatisfaction, frustrations, fears of the next day...

We intoxicate our minds with incessant "whys", without trying to understand the needs and sufferings of others, nor accept that things are "just like this", that they are in their best configuration for the time being.

The old monk's mind sees the essential thing to be done in the present moment: help the young girl cross the river. He does so without hesitation and then drops the event to regain peace of mind. This is letting go.

As for us, we often practise indifference to keep the mind serene, by justifying ourselves by various pretexts like this young monk. This attitude devoid of any compassion is not at all "Zen", on the contrary!

So, let us come back to the present moment and inspect our minds: What is the heavy lifting that we have dragged for so long without being able to let go? Why do we let it spoil all the wonderful moments of our daily life?

Let us drop our burden and be happy now!

85
THE ORDINARY SPIRIT

In ancient times, monks went from monastery to monastery to learn Zen from different masters.

One day, a monk went to the Zen master Zhao Zhou and asked him:

"Master, I have just arrived at the monastery. Teach me your zen».

Zhao Zhou asked him, "Have you eaten?"

The monk replied: "Yes, master"

Zhao Zhou then said to him: "Go wash your bowl!".

At these words, the monk was enlightened.

Years before, when Zhao Zhou was still a young monk, his master Nan Quan had taught him when he asked the same question to him: "The ordinary mind is the way!".

A while ago, a cartoon posted on Facebook reminded me of this Zen story. It featured a man sitting in front of posters on his desk asking his wife, "Honey, I'm looking for a slogan to support feminism. Do you have an idea?". She replied: "Go do the dishes!".

This truth makes people smile because it shows us how far we are from the right path. We speak of great works when we are unable to perform small tasks in full consciousness: breathing, walking, eating, talking, working...

We talk about love, compassion, soul greatness, light, heaven... but we often forget that these big words are contained in the small simple gestures of everyday life: giving an encouraging word, offering a compassionate smile, relieving his companion and his colleagues in daily tasks, give up victory in a quarrel, avoid hurting a weaker person, forgive the mistakes of others...

Recently, I discovered that the "postpartum blues", a syndrome of irritability, anxiety, vulnerability, and mood swings that afflicts many women after childbirth, is greatly reduced or even nonexistent when mothers are effectively assisted by their partners in the care of their newborn, as well as in household chores.

When one person asked Zen Master Seung Sahn this question, "What is love? He replied, "You take care of me, I take care of you, that's love".

Quite simply, that is the ordinary mind in ordinary tasks.

However, done with care and compassion, they can transform us into extraordinary people.

86
JEALOUSY

One of the worst feelings that can make us suffer throughout life is jealousy.

Few of us admit it, but no one escapes it, to varying degrees.

The history of mankind reveals several tragedies stemming from jealousy, the unhealthy form of which can lead to cruel or criminal acts. Genesis, the first book of the Bible, tells of a fratricidal crime between Cain and Abel, two brothers whose offerings of one find more favour in the sight of God than those of the other. Mythology leaves us a legacy of many stories on the theme of jealousy in love: Hera and Zeus, Eros and Psyche, Helen and Paris…

Daily, the various facts bring us stories of rivalry,

of revenge which end badly and leave an incalculable number of people in the suffering by ricochet.

A sociological study had shown that a wealthy person building his house in a neighbourhood where the neighbours are a little less wealthy than him considers himself happy. On the other hand, with the same standard of living, if he lives in a place where the neighbours are better off, he will feel miserable. We then understand that his well-being is not in relation to his wealth but to the feeling that he has more than others.

It is this comparison between self and others that creates jealousy. When born, the latter has the power to totally occupy our minds, obscure our thoughts, arouse our most violent emotions, and push us towards rash acts, sometimes with irreversible consequences.

What we call "love" also creates rivalries and conflicts. When we suffer in love, we are in fact dealing with its usurper, the "attachment" created by the ego.

Attachment creates the illusion of "property" ("he/she belongs to me"), arouses the reflex of defending one's "territory", rivalries, and therefore jealousy. Most of us fall victim to this illusion that turns love into hate and resentment.

However, in a "neither good nor bad" spiritual journey, jealousy is also an excellent yardstick for measuring the greatness of our ego. The less we trust ourselves, the less we love ourselves, the more we need to inflate our ego to prove to others that we are worthy and deserve their feelings and consideration.

The more ego grows, the more we compare ourselves to others and make jealousy intense.

Suffering inevitably sets in.

At this point, let us come back to our inner child and look at the wounds that jealousy has left there. Isn't now the time to drop all that mental load to start healing and being happy with ourselves?

87
PRIMUM NON NOCERE

Every medical student, from the start of his[8] studies, has necessarily heard this recommendation, hammered out throughout his course by various masters: "Primum non nocere!","First, do no harm!".

It sounds simple at first glance, but years of medical practice have helped me realise that this is a golden principle to be engraved in the minds of any caregiver.

Indeed, it is exceedingly difficult not to harm, when we have powerful double-edged weapons in our hands and sometimes must make decisions that can cost our patients dearly.

Simplistic minds may think that it is enough to

---

8 To increase fluency, the masculine form of all the personal pronouns (he/she), adjectives (his/her), and pronouns (him/her) were used. Of course, when it comes to women, they should their feminine forms.

practise so-called "soft" medicine to do no harm. However, missing out on a serious diagnosis or effective therapy can also lead to the loss of a sick person's chance of recovery.

Thus, to correctly respect this principle, each caregiver should relentlessly cultivate his medical knowledge to follow the evolution of science, without forgetting to seek to better understand the human being behind the pathologies, his sufferings, and his needs, to constantly keep a correct intention based on compassion and not on one's own interests.

At a higher level, because humanity suffers and each of us can be a caregiver for our neighbour, we should all apply the principle of "First, do no harm!" In our relationships with others.

Here the task is infinitely more difficult. Good intention is insufficient if it is not accompanied by a sufficiently broad knowledge of the human being. Didn't it say that "The road to hell is paved with good intentions"?

How many children have suffered from parents who thought they were doing well by giving them a severe and liberticidal education in the name of their personal pride, at the same time undermining all personal and creative initiative?

How many young people are destroyed by unattainable life goals imposed on them with emotional blackmail as a backdrop?

How many people around us have suffered from our clumsiness in words, in actions that were nevertheless intended for good on our part?

How much time and energy could we save without having to repair the damage caused by conflicts with those around us?

The work of the mind to "do no harm" is extremely rewarding. It will always help us to flush out the ego that lies dormant within us, ready to show off that we are good, altruistic and benevolent but in reality hungry for glory, victory and revenge inside.

It will help us to live in full awareness through our thoughts, our words and our actions, always based on compassion for all beings, especially the most fragile.

Then, we will have our ultimate reward: not to harm ourselves by the return of sticks, consequences of the injuries that we have inadvertently caused to others!

Primum non nocere, tunc vivere secundum naturam in omnibus, Amor.
First, do no harm, then live according to the nature of everything, Love.

88
THE SACRED DIMENSION OF OUR WORDS

In the Five Energy Movements (Wood, Fire, Earth, Metal and Water), speech is related to the energy of Fire. It is the manifestation of the Heart, the seat of the Spirit which is permanently connected with the original nature of everything. For this reason, the word carries a sacred dimension in Eastern spirituality.

The primary function of speech is communication. It allows us to express our desires, our needs and our intentions towards those around us. At a higher level, we use it to express our gratitude, our contentment but also our discomfort, our ailments through words, even our cries for help in the face of loneliness and distress felt.

Thus, the word acts like a wave that carries our

inner being to our surroundings, just like the eyes, our windows of the soul.

Who among us has never uttered regrettable words that deeply hurt others in times of anger, weariness or perdition? Yes, when our mind is overwhelmed with resentments, wounds of injustice, fear... , it tends to unload on others harsh, abusive words, without a valid reason for the interlocutor if he does not look deeply at the suffering of the one who uttered them.

Who among us has never lied to avoid facing a predicament? Yes, when fear invades us, we tend to react like a child who protects himself with his small means against possible reprisals which are felt to be terrifying.

Who among us has never used the word to judge, condemn and threaten others without thinking for a moment that it could mark him/her for life? In my consultations, I have often heard from elderly people who still suffer from harsh judgments from their parents from 50, 60 years ago! Unlike physical injuries, those inflicted by words can take much longer to heal, if ever.

Who among us has not at least once betrayed his own words by revealing secrets that could harm others, spreading false rumours to hurt, sowing discord, achieving the desired result, deceiving those who trust him?

If we take a little time to revise our conscience, we will see all the damage we have done to others, intentionally or negligently. At the same time, we could review our vocabulary: does it know a lot of terms that translate as contempt, pride, aggression, mockery, brutality, rudeness? They should be seen as loaded guns that we always have at hand. One day, we will use it and hurt those around us.

Let us give back to the word its sacred dimension by using it in wisdom and compassion to console, help and encourage.

The Fire movement being linked to the Heart, the seat of love and joy, the light of our words will spring if they are sincere, modest, and benevolent.

And let us not forget the power of silence, the Yin side of speech, sometimes more valuable than all possible words.

"If you meet a person who deserves your words, but you do not speak up, you lose the person.

If you meet a person who does not deserve your words, but you speak up, you lose the word.

A wise man loses neither the person nor the word "

Confucius

89
PICK UP THE PRESENT MOMENT

With the beauty of the past that leaves its mark
Shadows and lights,
Joys and sorrows,
Awakening and ignorance,
With the beauty of what is to come
Fragility and strength,
Doubts and hope,
Fear and confidence,

Look inside you.
Everything is here,
Behind many faces
On the move and unchanging
Always
Forever
In a single instant
In one space
Here
and now

90
LAUGH, SMILE AND LOTS OF LAUGHTER

Yesterday, a patient I have known for a very long time came for a consultation. He is a cheerful person who loves to tell jokes. He always reserves his best jokes for me every time we meet, forcing me to have some backing. This time, a little story put us in endless laughter, including tears, nasal discharge, and contracture pain in the abdominal muscles. There was nothing masks could do to hide our joys. We could not finish an entire sentence without breaking out of laughter in the middle. I think the other patients must have heard us all the way to the waiting room.

I have to tell you, after this happy episode after a hard day, I thought to myself, "Ah, it's been a while since I laughed so hard! It feels good ". That is true. When we laugh, it is like our brains are cleaning up.

He takes his magic broom and instantly drives away our worries, our stresses, all our problems and all our other negative emotions. Laughter thus invigorates our immune system and makes us stronger and more resistant to the shocks of life.

It is such a simple thing that we often forget. According to researchers, when we were children, we laughed up to 300 times a day, often for no reason. As adults, we only laugh 20 times a day at most! By becoming "grown-ups", serious and concerned about our future, we lose our innocence and our spontaneous joy. As a result, some professionals have developed laughter therapy that is practised in groups. The latter has even entered hospitals to reduce pain and stress in patients and caregivers.

Laughter has a curious capacity: it is contagious! I will always remember a TV show where Henry Salvador, a happy French singer, demonstrated this power: he laughed for about a minute and gradually everyone around him followed him until they laughed. I still remember my condition at that time, folded in half...

So, in these times when our smile, an "under-laughter" hidden by our masks, might be invisible, let us give it a voice and tears in our eyes, so many messages of tenderness, remedies against disaster, gloom, and deadly atmospheres.

Let us laugh, smile, laugh... without moderation and bring our joy to the world! 🙂

91
DYING IS JUST RETURNING TO ONE'S HOME

Yesterday, I had a rewarding conversation with a patient at the end of the consultation day.

He is a learned and very human university professor. He is interested in several areas of knowledge, even if they are not his own expertise.

Like me, he has been educated in religion from an early age, but all the religious concepts instilled in him are not enough to remove the fear of death from him. He was asking my opinion on this great passage which seems to be terrifying for many people.

Therefore, I took the liberty of giving him my personal point of view, stressing that it in no way constitutes a criticism of religions and practitioners.

Let us try to adopt a purely rational view, without any belief. Let us call "A" the total amount of atoms existing on earth since life began to settle there. Apart from small variations by the few stardust and meteorites that occasionally land on our planet, "A" could be considered an almost invariable number.

The law of conservation of masses during the change of state of matter by Antoine Lavoisier states that "nothing is lost, nothing is created, everything is transformed". For millions of years, the human population has continued to grow. From 600 million at the beginning of the 18th century, we have grown to 7.8 billion today.

As "A" remains invariable, our development should undoubtedly come at the expense of other species, both animals and plants.

If we mark an atom to follow its movement from one living being to another since the dawn of time, we can see that it has been present everywhere, borrowed, and then returned billions and billions of times, without ever "dying".

Thus, our whole body is made of permanent recycling, by interaction with all beings, without anything really belonging to us definitively.

This is the "hardware" part, the material of our body.

As for the "software" that represents our mind?

If we leave the belief in the "individual soul" aside to remain rational, we can talk about our consciousness, which is highly developed in human beings. However, objectively we cannot deny that it is shaped by a collective consciousness from our childhood, after years of education and formatting by elders, learning from knowledge accumulated by elders, d 'experiences of life and of exchanges with others, of deconditioning and changes of direction... to arrive at an illusion of individuality today.

So, what I call "me" or "we" at this moment has already existed forever in different forms and different lives can never disappear but only travel through time and space.

After the conversation, we parted with a burst of laughter, thinking we had met already somewhere in the past, maybe not so distant, thanks to our "permanent deaths".

The fear of death thus left in silence.

Dying is just returning to one's home.

The waves die, never the ocean.

92
ONE OF THE WORST EXPERIENCES

Human beings inevitably go through many experiences in their life, but one of their greatest fears is feeling lonely.

Indeed, he is not programmed to live alone.

During intrauterine life, the foetus, in interaction with its mother, has already received floods of sensations that will become biological traces of its memory, of its memories. He dreamed and generated many images before being born, which will be used in the future construction of his psyche.

After birth, he needs interactions with the world around him, through visual and physical contact as well as the other senses. He separates himself from others and individualises himself while learning from them and integrating their influences into his own characteristics. The presence of his parents is so decisive that even absent, they remain buried in him like landmarks that soothe his emotions, console him, and show him the way to follow.

In adulthood, he still has a "child nucleus" that is weak, limited, and incomplete. As a result, anxiety or even fear of loneliness always remains present in him.

Some time ago, I found the lyrics to a song I wrote when I was around 25, in a great moment of distress:

"Loneliness, I hate you when you hold me.

Loneliness, you sow uncertainty in my path.

Loneliness, you leave and come back like a chorus.

Loneliness, I beg you, at least let me go tonight".

Loneliness is just a feeling of being misunderstood just when we need help, understanding, attention or affection. As a result, we can be surrounded while feeling alone.

Even the greatest of this world have known this feeling of distress. Before he died on the cross, Jesus cried out, *"My God, my God, why have you forsaken me?"* (Matthew 27,46).

While writing my doctoral thesis on *"In search of the predictive profile of suicides according to periods of life"*, I noticed that loneliness was particularly present in the elderly who commit suicide, thinking that their life no longer made sense because it becomes useless and no longer interests anyone.

But then, do we have a remedy to fight loneliness? Of course, but at different levels!

At the simplest level, let us review our behaviour

towards others. This is often the cause of our loneliness.

A bloated "me" often leads to rejection from those around him who prefer to avoid being subjected to conflicts, reproaches, aggressive attitudes, unfriendly words…

We cannot claim the attention and affection of others without being caring and loving with those around us ourselves. It is a simple but often forgotten truth.

At a higher level, our mind must strive for wholeness. This quest is that of a lifetime. Fullness implies no longer having existential questions to ask oneself constantly, including one's own path as well as the workings of the world around us. Wholeness arises from the equanimous mind that accepts events "as they are" with their bright and dark sides. It brings about a serenity quickly regained during the passage of the storms of life.

With spiritual fullness, we will never feel alone as we are permanently connected with the entire Universe.

Loneliness will then become just an illusory feeling.

93
FROM CAUSES TO EFFECTS

Today I welcomed a young man in a sorry state. After getting angry two days ago during an argument, he punched a wall hard and fractured several bones in his hand with sagging skin and severe bleeding. He was treated in traumatology but suffered a lot despite the various treatments prescribed.

In Eastern spirituality, this is called karma, a cause-and-effect relationship. No one is there to judge whether their act is right or wrong. Only the consequences are present, in their dark (pain) and luminous face (lesson on the need to control your emotions).

This story is an example of simple karma (one cause, one effect).

In reality, the effects can occur in a chain. When we watch the news in the newspaper or on television, we can see that an assault or murder of a person causes suffering to many of their loved ones, and this for an exceptionally long time, sometimes for a lifetime.

On an even greater scale, the entry of a country at war can create disastrous consequences for hundreds of thousands of people and their families.

Humanity and all living beings are linked by different karmas.

When a person is saved from death or illness, his loved ones are happy and relieved. When we witness a love or compassion story, thousands of hearts can bloom with tears of joy.

Thus, from small actions, we can create a hell or a paradise for our neighbours because of the reactions which follow one another in a long karmic chain.

This observation awakens us to the importance of each of our thoughts, our words and every one of our actions.

Let us put a lot of gentleness, kindness, and care not to hurt.

Let us relieve them of the weight of our enlarged ego. Let us not think about "good" or "bad" but just do what needs to be done.

Let us not be afraid sometimes to be daring, like trying to grow flowers in the desert, or pacifying wolves by being nice sheep.

Contrary to what many of us have always believed, victory does not belong to the strongest or the fiercest, but to those who always know how to create favourable karmas.

No door will be closed to them.

No obstacle will be able to stop them.

94
WHY SO MUCH HATES?

This morning, a Facebook friend posted this question in the comments of one of my posts: "Why so much 'evil' on earth, why so many monsters? ".

I am sure that many of us are also asking this question which deserves reflection.

All religions will give us a clear and simple answer: "Evil is the work of the devil! As opposed to the "good" that comes from God. The freedom to choose is placed in the heart of every human, it is up to them to move towards the light or to switch to the dark side. This answer satisfies most men, although it is based solely on belief, passed down from generation to generation.

What about Eastern spirituality?

To understand this, we have to go back in time, to the time when life begins to appear on earth, in the form of bacteria, a microorganism with a single cell. Although it does not yet have a nucleus, this archaebacterium has a membrane that constitutes the limits of its "self" and which separates it from the environment in which it lives, considered as "non-self". To ensure her survival, she will seek whatever is favourable to her, the "pro-self" and at the same time avoid whatever is unfavourable to her, the "anti-self".

Man arrives on earth a few billion years later. Although he is a conscious being, endowed with a superior intelligence, he still maintains this self-preservation reflex, the survival instinct, the purpose of which is to save the soldier's "ego".

In Eastern spirituality, this limit of the "self" is an illusion because no being can live alone and partitioned off, without constantly interacting with the entire universe, whether with the cosmos (sun, moon among others), other humans, animals, plants, and minerals. The illusion of the self is like seeing each wave as being fixed, unchanging and different from each other in their characteristics, without understanding that all waves are in fact only manifestations of the ocean.

From this was born ignorance, the source of "pro-self" and "anti-self". She creates egotistical visions, egotistical thoughts and egotistical opinions which make humanity believe itself to be its own enemy to envy and kill each other.

There is no evil, no monster, just ignorance. We only need to wake up to understand that love will be revealed when ignorance has receded, for it is our original nature.

Let us bring in the light of wisdom to light up the darkness of ignorance and love will shine forth. This was to be demonstrated.

95
RÉSOLUTIONS

A friend on Facebook once posted this mantra of the day:

"Love is my law

Peace is my refuge

Experience is my school

Determination is my strength

Authenticity is my pillar

Humour is my antidote

Difficulty is my milestone

Pain is my alarm

Wisdom is my way "

It's a very beautiful text, indisputably, but still very

much linked to "me" and "mine".

Imagine removing the "my", isn't the motto more calming?

"Compassion is the rule
Peace is home
Experience is teaching
Determination is strength
Authenticity is a pillar
Humour is antidote
Difficulty is hardship
Pain is sentinel
Wisdom is way "

Just by removing the boundaries that separate my opinion from those of others, the "little me" will be diluted in Emptiness and peace will come.

96
WHAT IS A CHILLI?

Imagine that we should explain what a chilli pepper is to a blind person who has never seen it.

We can use our encyclopaedic knowledge and explain to him that chilli is a fruit of five species of plants of the genus Capsicum of the Solanaceae family, used as a condiment or vegetable. We might also add that the capsaicin it contains plays an interesting fat-burning role in limiting the risk of obesity.

We know that red peppers are stronger than green peppers, but since we do not know how to explain the colours to them, we will refrain from discussing this delicate detail.

Instead, we will tell him the story of this fruit, teaching him that chilli has been part of the Americas diet for at least 9,500 years and that it is currently mainly produced by India at 38.7%. of world production.

To be closer to the details, we can describe its shape, its firm consistency like pepper and its very strong pungent taste that burns the tongue and the mouth.

After that, we will be happy to have taught him everything about chilli.

Indeed, our interlocutor now knows a lot about chilli, but only through our story. It is his trust in our words.

On the other hand, if we put a chilli in his hand so that he can smell and taste it, he will know the chilli for himself. This is his personal experience with chilli peppers.

At that point, he will no longer need to believe, for he has "met" the chilli! His faith thus becomes useless.

It is the same when we try to explain to others what is inexplicable, invisible and non-palpable, such as the notion of God. We create a belief but not a real encounter.

Only spirituality, a personal journey through multiple difficulties with perseverance and sincerity, will allow each of us to experience the ultimate reality, an encounter that will change our lives forever.

97
ILLUMINATION

When I first started learning about Buddhism, I read a lot of Zen tales without understanding their meaning, especially those that relate to the enlightenment of Zen monks.

Here is one about awakening a nun:

Chiyono is a simple woman from the countryside. She took refuge in a nunnery to serve and live her spiritual life. Desiring more than anything to understand the essence of the teachings, she went to her superior and asked her: "I cannot read or trace ideograms; I am not good at studying and have to do so many household chores every day. Could I, under these conditions, understand and practise the path of the Buddhas?". The latter reassured her by telling her that when the time is right, everything will be revealed to her suddenly.

One full moon evening, she went down to the spring to fill her buckets with water, which she brought back to the monastery. On the way home, when she gazed at the reflection of the moon dancing on the surface of the water, the bottom of the bucket suddenly gave way. The water and the moon immediately disappeared.

She instantly achieved enlightenment and composed this poem:

"From odds and ends, I tried to patch up the old bucket

And then the bottom gave way.

More water in the bucket. No more moon in the water.

The mind becomes empty of everything".

What had she suddenly understood?

In our daily life, we attach ourselves to many things, material or immaterial, such as teachings, symbols, traditions, beliefs, ideologies... They reassure us by their presence, so much so that we rely on them for us feel secure and are so afraid of losing them: "What would become of me if I had no more money, no more love, no respect from others, no more fame, no more family, no more community, capacity, beauty, health, no more hope, more no faith...?"

All these things are like the golden reflections of the moon on the surface of the water, so beautiful, and peaceful. How lucky for us to have them right now.

The time will come when the bottom of the bucket

gives way under the weight of the water, taking with it all our precious attachments. For most of us, it is the catastrophe, the great loss, the nothingness of our life.

However, for those who walk in spiritual search, this moment can be the one of their enlightenment. Indeed, the reflection of the moon has disappeared with the water, but we just have to look up to contemplate the real moon, to look around us to see its light in every tree, on every leaf, on every stone, and to realise that we have always walked under its light.

Only the illusion is gone, giving way to the splendour of reality that our blind eyes had never seen before.

Enlightenment is nothing out of the ordinary. It is just an awakening and an acceptance of letting go of all concepts that clutter the mind.

We could then travel freely between heaven and earth.

98
THE GOD OF SPINOZA

Historian Simon Veille, in an article written for *Le Monde des religions*, recounted this anecdote about Einstein, the famous Jewish physicist known around the world for his theory of relativity with his famous formula $E = MC^2$:

"When asked if he believes in God, Einstein replies: I believe in the God of Spinoza, who reveals himself in the harmony of all that exists but not in a God who would be preoccupied with destiny and the acts of human beings."

Baruch Spinoza is a 17th-century Dutch philosopher. His works maintain a critical relationship with the traditional positions of the monotheistic religions of Judaism, Christianity, and Islam.

In his philosophical work Ethica written in Latin between 1661 and 1675, published on his death in 1677 and banned the following year, he wrote:

"I don't know if God actually spoke but if he did, here's what I think he would say to the believer:

Stop praying and kicking yourself in the chest!

What I want you to do is go out into the world to enjoy your life.

I want you to have fun, sing, relax... enjoy everything I have done for you.

Stop going to those dark cold temples that you built yourself and say it is my house!

My house is in the mountains, in the woods, rivers and lakes.

This is where I live with you and express my love for you.

Stop accusing me of your miserable life,

I never told you there was anything wrong with you, that you were a sinner, that your sexuality or joy was a bad thing!

So do not blame me for everything they told you to believe.

Stop rehashing sacred reading that has nothing to do with me.

If you cannot read me at dawn, in a landscape, in the eyes of your friend, your wife, your man, in your son's eyes...

You will not find me in a book!

Stop being scared.

I do not judge you. I do not criticise you. I do not come home angry, and I do not punish.

I am pure love... I filled you with passions, limitations, pleasures, feelings, needs, inconsistencies... and I gave you free will...

How can I blame you if you answer something I put in you?

How can I punish you for being who you are, if I am the one who made you?

Do you really think I could create a place to burn all my kids who behave badly, for the rest of eternity?

What kind of God can do this?

If I were like this, I would not deserve to be respected.

If I just wanted to be revered, I would have filled the earth with dogs...

Respect your fellow people and do not do what you do not want for yourself.

All I am asking is that you pay attention to your life and let your free will be your guide.

You and nature will have a single body... so do not believe you have power over it.

You are a part of her.

Take care of her and she will take care of you. I put in you and made everything good for you and made it difficult to access what is not.

Do not put your genius into looking for what is bad for this balance.

It is up to you to keep this balance intact.

Nature knows how to keep it, just do not trouble it!

I made you absolutely free.

You are absolutely free to create a paradise or hell

in your life.

I cannot tell you if there is anything after this life, but I can give you some advice,

Stop believing in me this way,

Believing is guessing, guessing, guessing.

I do not want you to believe in me, I want you to feel me in you.

May you feel me in you when you take care of your sheep, when you pet your dog, when you touch your little girl, when you fall in the river...

Express your joy and get used to taking just what you need!

The only thing for sure is that you are here, that you are alive, that this world is full of wonders... and in all these wonders you are able to know exactly what you really need.

Do not look for me outside,

You will not find me...

I am here... Nature,

The cosmos... It's me".

Spinoza's ideas move away from Western theology to join Eastern cosmology.

It just goes to show that the great spiritual thinkers all come together at the same summit, after years of climbing different mountain paths.

99
COMPLICATED BUT SIMPLE AND VICE VERSA

Zen language is often obscure and contradictory to the uninitiated, but when understanding suddenly arrives, the light that shoots into it is often blinding and renders sight.

Here is a little story that illustrates these words:

In China during the Tang Dynasty, there was a great scholar named Ly. Legend has it that he read over ten thousand books and gave him the nickname "Mr Ly of ten thousand books".

One day, he went to consult a Zen master and asked him the following question: "The Vimalakirti Sutra [a famous Buddhist Sutra] says that Mount Meru may contain a grain of mustard and a grain of mustard may contain Mount Meru. I would like to believe the first statement, but the second is implausible. How can a small grain of mustard contain all of Mount Meru?"

The master replied: "It seems to me that you are called 'Mr. Ly of ten thousand books'. How could your little skull hold ten thousand books?".

The big problem of our time is that we can no longer see anything but unsubtle, "gross" and obvious things, which follow a simple logic that anyone can accept. As soon as it comes to a more subtle area that escapes our Cartesian reasoning and comprehension, we are ready to think "this is too fuzzy!", Or even "crazy!".

However, the realm of spirituality is a subtle realm. It lies well beyond belief and non-belief, frequent subjects of sterile debate.

When we are in belief, we blindly trust what we have been taught without ever doubting it.

True faith is to question all beliefs and experience yourself through a patient and sincere inner journey. This quest will bring us to an awakening, an enlightenment that will bring us face to face with the ultimate reality.

At that point, belief becomes useless since we will become One with it.

One day someone told me, "I have spent my life looking for God and I still cannot find him!". I replied: "Ah, it's like this Zen riddle, complicated but simple at the same time. It is just a maths problem to think about. You have faith; therefore you are surely thinking: "I am in God". But in your prayers, you also think "God is in me".

If A is included in B and at the same time B is included in A, what can you deduce?"

If you do not understand it, that is okay.

When spring comes, the grass will sprout on its own.

100
THE ULTIMATE TRUTH

A young monk asked his master:

- Master, what is the ultimate truth?
- Go ask the tree in the garden, he will teach you!

This morning, the weather is magnificent. In my garden, nature continues to beautify itself, to adorn itself with colourful garments of dazzling colours. The bees quietly forage on the flowers of the plum tree, their legs loaded with pollen, under a soft and benevolent sun. They are so carefree. Nothing special is happening in their world. It is still a spring like so many others, meanwhile, humans are dying by the tens of thousands all over the globe due to the pandemic. The bright future gives way to obscurity which gradually expands each day, leaving so much suffering and grief in its path. One only needs to turn on the television to see the stark contrast between the human world and that of all other living beings.

Not so long ago, it was the other way around. It is as if men and extra-human nature live in parallel universes, completely oblivious to each other.

So, I went to the tree in the garden to ask him about the ultimate truth.

In response, he invited me to take a long journey into the past, 3.5 billion years ago, where our two universes were not yet separated from each other, where we were both single-cell beings.

Still, a few billion years ago, we both existed, he and I, only as stardust.

Crossing the threshold of the Big Bang, the starting point of the appearance of our universe, we enter a still emptiness where no words, no concept could describe, having appeared much later.

And there, in overwhelming silence, the tree whispered in my ear: "We are the ultimate truth!"

101
DESCENT INTO HELL

One of the most striking anecdotes about Zen master Seung Sahn is told by one of his close disciples.

One day, the master and his more alert students set off to visit Las Vegas. As they walked through the streets, they noticed that their master had suddenly disappeared. The latter reappeared among them with hands full of slot machine tokens. He distributed a good number of them to everyone, saying, "Go play at the casino, have fun!".

His disciples were stunned, wondering if their master had suddenly gone mad asking them to break the precepts of monastic life.

Seung Sahn explained to them, "You know these

places can be hell for those who fail to get out. If you want to help them, you must agree to go down to hell to see and understand their reasons. So go play!".

Thereby, a few years ago, I spent a few evening hours gambling in a Las Vegas casino (and ended up losing all my chips). I had noticed the haggard demeanour of a lady, glued to her chair at one in the morning in front of a slot machine that promised players a million-dollar jackpot. Every time her hand mechanically pressed the button, five dollars went up in smoke. But in her eyes, there was no reaction, as if there was nothing more to lose unless a miracle happened. In a little over a quarter of an hour, a thousand dollars was gone, but she was still playing. There is a great chance that it will be ruined and in pain for years to come. I was there, at this place and at that time, to witness the hell of addiction and its immense power.

Thus, the more we seek to understand deeply the heart of the human being with his sufferings, the more we open our own towards tolerance and compassion for all beings, without judgement or condemnation. Seeing and confronting the suffering of others allows us to mature and let go of many illusions out of ignorance.

To walk with others in no way means to bear all their sufferings nor to take pleasure in their vices. It is simply a matter of being present in the key moments of one's life, between his paradises and his hells.

Let us be without fear. Love is beyond all precepts.

With compassion and egoless wisdom, we will not be exposed to any danger until the end of our journey.

102
IT WAS BETTER BEFORE!

"It is decadence, children no longer obey, language is damaged, morals are breaking down… ".

"The youth of today are rotten to the core, evil, irreligious and lazy. It will never be like the youth of the past and will be incapable of preserving our civilization ".

"I have no hope for the future of our country if the young people of today are to be the leaders of tomorrow because they are unbearable, oblivious and even frightening. If the future of our people is in the hands of today's frivolous youth, there is cause for despair. This youth behaves with a truly intolerable complacency. She thinks she has science in it. When I was young, we were taught good manners and the respect we owe our parents. But the new generation *keeps arguing and wants to be right. It is a fact that young people are extremely carefree"*.

Contrary to what you might have thought, these are not current press articles or the words of any contemporary celebrity.

The first quote is from Ipuwer of Giza, a sage from Pharaonic Egypt who lived 3000 years BCE. It is cited by Polybius, a Greek historian living around 200-120 years BC.

The second is found on a Babylonian clay tablet estimated to be over 3000 years old.

The latter is taken from the work "The Labors and Days of Hesiod" by Thebes, a Greek poet who lived in the mid-8th century BC.

We can see that since the dawn of time, each generation has always tended to consider its own as a benchmark and to treat future generations with disdain, accused of laxity, disrespect, decadence and therefore destroying the future.

Very often I hear people complaining: "In my day, it wasn't like that… " or "It was better before… ".

However, if we look objectively at the history of mankind with the dark periods it went through, who among us would like to go back to the middle ages, to the dark times when the law was strictly in the hands of the strongest? who held all the powers, at the time of slavery, of the world wars with the extermination of the innocent, at the time of prohibitions without valid reason which shattered lives?

With the development of media and social networks, the vices that were previously hidden behind taboos have come to light and show that the elders are hardly better than the current generation.

Compared to the past, although our world is far from perfect, it is evolving in the right direction, towards the awakening of consciousness, equality between men and the management of power relations to create a more peaceful, fairer world. And this, thanks to the younger generations who continue to continuously improve the legacy left by the elders.

Their tasks are not the easiest. Since 1950, the world's population has more than tripled, from 2.5 billion to 7.8 billion. Without a wake-up call on overconsumption, the earth's resources will soon be insufficient for all. Environmental pollution is another big problem, drinking water for which has become a matter of survival in many parts of the world. Wars of ideology continue to hurt millions of human beings, who only dream of being able to live in freedom.

Maybe you think I am too optimistic, but I believe a lot in the youth of future generations.

I am sure they will be able to work for a fairer, freer, cleaner world.

I would not go back and live in the past for the world. Besides, I just destroyed the blueprints of my De Lorean, the time machine.

103
THE RIGHT QUESTION TO ASK

Man is an evolved animal. Like all other living things, he has basic needs. However, he is endowed with awareness, intelligence, and wisdom, which allows him to move in the right direction towards self-realisation. Psychologist Abraham Maslow prioritised human needs in a pyramid that has five levels:

- Physiological needs are found at the base of the pyramid: to breathe, to eat, to rest, to sleep, to eliminate, to have neuromuscular and sexual activity.

- Once these needs have been met, man accesses level two of the pyramid, that of psychological needs: feeling safe, finding family and professional stability, accessing property.

- The social needs of the individual belong to level three: the feeling of belonging (to a family, a group of friends, to society, etc.), emotional needs: to be recognized, esteemed, and loved by others.

- At level four of the pyramid, a man works his mind and aims for self-esteem. He needs to accept himself, to be useful and independent. He explores different fields of knowledge, scientific and artistic.

- The top of the pyramid, level five, is that of self-realisation. Through his past experiences, man acquires maturity and wisdom. He turns to others to share his spiritual fulfilment, his realisation. He finally becomes what he "is".

Life is built out of successive choices. At each of its crossroads, we must decide which new direction to take. Some of us will never leave the first floors of the pyramid and will continue to rise even if our needs are largely met. Others will target the upper floors by enriching their cultural and spiritual life.

Imagine that the top, the one that represents self-actualisation, is the top of a mountain. To get there, we can follow several different paths. There are major roads used by the greatest number because they are easy to access and do not require special effort. Other trails are much narrower. Some slopes are steep and icy, but they lead directly to the summit.

There is no such thing as a universal path. Each traveller will have to create their own. However, only certain directions will lead us to happiness, such as the path of wisdom and compassion, where every human works for the happiness of others.

So, every day we ask ourselves this unique good question: "Am I happy / fulfilled?". If the answer is positive, let us continue our journey. Otherwise, a review of priorities is called for.

Our happiness is built little by little through successive choices that are never perfectly judicious or totally wrong.

As a result, they sublimate our lives into an infinitely difficult art.

104
BALANCED

The human body has the amazing ability to maintain homeostasis automatically. As soon as a biological constant or a physiological state leaves its zone of normality, it will quickly restore balance thanks to variations in hormones and neurotransmitters.

However, the mental activity of the human mind is so tortuous and incessant that it creates uncontrollable emotions which regularly hamper this fragile harmony.

With anxiety, sadness, and fear, our brains work sluggishly. When depression lasts for a long time, the very size of the brain is reduced by the rarefaction of neurons, with a marked decrease in neural connections.

Our loss of balance becomes visible in our

daily life: the appetite goes away. We eat to fill an existential void rather than to nourish our bodies.

Insomnia sets in. We no longer recover during our sleep, we become drowsy and tired during the day.

Anger drives away serenity and leaves room for mental agitation, even over-excitement in words and actions.

Frustration deepens the existential void and calls for addiction to fill the imbalance. We devote ourselves to alcohol, tobacco, drugs, compulsive shopping, pleasures of the senses...

Significant imbalances lead to a degradation of the body, a decrease in defences and make the bed of diseases.

Also, we must be vigilant and keep our minds as well as possible to live as long as possible in happiness.

According to the physiology of traditional Chinese medicine, we can follow the five energetic movements to maintain our balance:

- With the **Wood** movement, let us keep clairvoyance on our life path and prepare our projects with intelligence and patience. Let us accept each moment as the best possible configuration, whether it be bright or dark.

- With the **Fire** movement, let us maintain joy in our hearts and do not hesitate to share it with those around us to maintain the ambient optimism in all circumstances. At the same time, let us be careful not to seek pleasure at all costs.

- With the **Earth** movement, let us share our resources with others when possible, to restore a more just world: knowledge, wisdom, compassion, help, consolation, support...

   - With the **Metal** movement, let us never stop learning, cultivating ourselves to raise our vision to higher levels, allowing greater tolerance through a better understanding of the human being. Let us also not forget moments of mindful meditation to return to our original essence.

   - With the **Water** movement, let us forge the will never to be discouraged in the face of failures, sometimes terrifying trials of life, to always get up after a fall and move forward in serenity and confidence.

   Any athlete will confirm it to us: knowing how to keep balance is a long-term job, with hours and hours of training.

   The same is true for the balance of the mind. Lasting serenity can only be achieved with a spiritual journey that will unfold over years, if not decades.

   It is never too late.

   Now is the time to sublimate our art of living.

105
INFINITE PATIENCE

If you can have "drip" coffee in Vietnam, you will know that it is almost an art.

The ground coffee is packed between two mini strainers. Hot water is poured over it and the coffee drips into the glass. One could imagine the drop of water meeting the coffee, soaking up its flavour and then uniting with it to become coffee before falling into the glass.

All of this takes time, sometimes a lot of time, which involves patience.

The cheesemaker and the winegrower have understood this for a long time. It takes months or even years for milk to turn into good cheese and grapes into good wine, not to mention all the ideal conditions necessary for processing to take place.

Slowness, patience... are the Yin side of each

achievement. It is often invisible but is always present behind what is visible on the outside, the Yang face: excellence, speed, efficiency, performance.

Indeed, unlike money, knowledge cannot be acquired overnight. It takes us years of effort, of repetitions, of revisions, of adjustments, of experiences, therefore of will and patience, before knowledge becomes ours.

So, it is with the wisdom that must slowly be born out of a long personal history with painful experiences of the past which serve as a breeding ground for awakening, a determination beyond fear, sincerity of the heart and a relentless training of the soul. mind.

In the history of Zen, when the Fifth Patriarch Hong Ren gave his bowl and tunic, symbols of the passing of power, to the future Sixth Patriarch Hui Neng after confirming his enlightenment, he recommended that he not teach during the 5 following years. Although the awakening is there, it still takes time to experience it, to confront it with the different trials of daily life, so that its teachings really come from its own understanding and not from what has caused it. been instilled.

Yet very often we want to eat a fruit that is still green and then wince in disgust or want to force a result and then be disappointed when it is disappointing.

Let us be patient. Like water that turns into coffee, milk into cheese or grapes into wine, this Yin time of withdrawal, of preparation is not at all useless, on the contrary.

It forms the foundations of what we will be in the future, solid or shaky.

Our life is an art, and all art takes time.

106
LETTER TO MY DAUGHTER

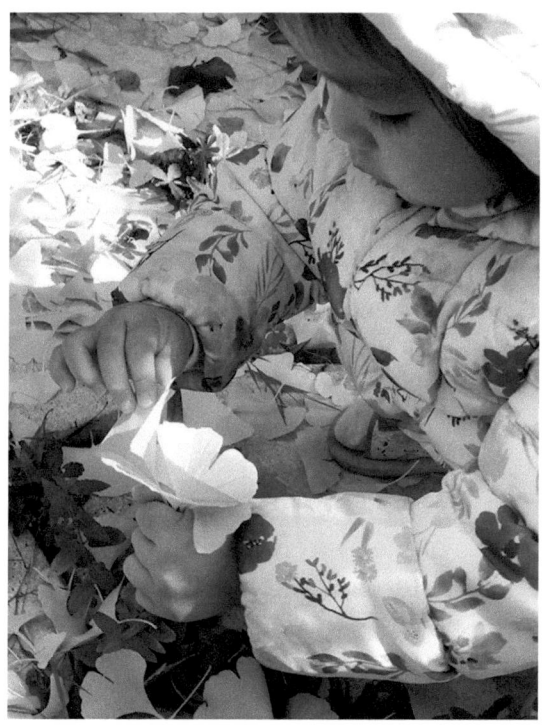

My darling,

As of this writing, you are only two years old. One day you will become a woman and run your life on your own without me. I take the time before this day arrives to share with you some life experiences, some of which have cost me years of my youth and sometimes even more.

This will not keep you from the same mistakes since your life should be based on your own experiences and not on your entire belief in my teachings. However, the day it does happen, you might be able to console yourself by telling yourself that your dad went through the same thing and did well, so do not panic!

With the education you have received, I have no doubt that you will succeed professionally and become an intelligent and well-educated woman.

However, all of this will not be enough to make you happy.

As you move around the world of educated and intelligent people, you will notice that the difference between them will only be seen in their intelligence of heart, but it is a fundamental difference!

Know how to recognize it through their behaviour towards those around them: if they have the same respect for an important personality, a boss, a service agent or even a child, you can see it as a sign of a beautiful person.

The intelligence of the heart is manifested in words that are compassionate, moderate, and righteous, promises always kept, actions without bragging, stepping forward to receive praise, but genuinely good and selfless.

Avoid toxic relationships that generate endless arguments and conflicts. They can pull you away from your loving nature and draw you into unnecessary and destructive wars. Take your time to appreciate the person who will be your travelling companion for a long time.

Give great importance to your personal achievement because it will make you happy forever, despite the ups and downs that you will encounter in your life.

Refrain from judging others but only strive to improve yourself every day. Your words and actions should always come from a good intention to avoid causing avoidable suffering around you.

Learn to be self-sufficient, not only financially, but above all emotionally. Do not leave your happiness in the hands of anyone. You are the only person who can make you happy or unhappy. Your independence is precious and must be preserved at all costs.

Be strong without crushing anyone or becoming proud, persuasive without wanting to win at all costs with reason because sometimes, keeping feelings and a relationship are much more precious.

Always keep a balanced mind in the face of successes and failures. Use your painful experiences to progress, not to regress. Be a good gardener who knows how to get a beautiful garden by turning manure into flowers.

Finally, trust your karma. Whatever happens to you is the best. Maybe you have not seen it yet, but you will understand it in the future.

Always keep the path of bodhisattva, the path of compassion, and become a light that enlightens and a source of warmth that comforts.

By your realisation, I will remain in you, everywhere and always.

And never forget to be happy!

Your father who loves you

BEFORE LEAVING

    Before closing this book and walking towards awakening, I wish everyone success

    To transform our outer world as beautiful as our inner world,

    To transform our inner world as beautiful as that of our dreams and

    To charge our dreams of love and compassion for all beings.

Winter 2020